WOMAN
REPOSITION YOURSELF

*Reveal your design
and don't let anything
steal your essence*

WOMAN
REPOSITION YOURSELF

Yesenia Then

WOMAN REPOSITION YOURSELF

© Yesenia Then, 2023

Phone 829.731.4205 and 809.508.7788

Email: www.yeseniathen.org

ISBN: 979-8987-9144-0-3

Publishing & Distribution: RENACER 1 CORP

Edit & Translations: Ofelia Perez

Cover and layout design: Pablo Montenegro

Printed in Santo Domingo, DN Dominican Republic.

Dedication

To all the women who, instead of being killed by their oppressors, decide to build castles with the stones they throw at them.

Acknowledgments

To my greatest Love, for Whom I live and exist, my Owner, Lord and Savior Jesus Christ. Besides giving meaning to my life by assigning it a purpose, He gives me the grace, strength, and courage to conquer it.

To my children, my treasures Maiky and Andy, for their support, accompaniment, and the great courage shown in each of the processes we have had to face.

To my invaluable work team, who, without sparing any effort, with so much passion, dedication, and care, is dedicated to the realization of each project that the Lord tells us to carry out.

To my personal assistant, Ana Karen Morillo, for her hard and tireless work, faithfulness, and continuous support not only in my ministry but in every aspect of my life.

Table of Contents

Foreword

S ome people have a platform that sustains them from the beginning, and it is glorious to see how they honor this beatitude. However, there is greater Glory to the Lord when everything starts with a substance called FAITH. This is the case of the author of this biblical gem.

In her fourth literary child, "WOMAN REPOSITION YOURSELF," Pastor Then lets us see the essence of God in some women who have been questioned by many preachers and scholars of the Holy Scriptures due to their biblical role—making it clear that, even in the worst cases, there is always a common denominator called: GOD'S PURPOSE.

I must confess that "WOMAN REPOSITION YOURSELF" is a work that I highly recommend, and I consider that we should all read, especially women. It is impressive how each page is full of revelations and hidden treasures through the lives of women who managed to consolidate great purposes that were simple for their environment:

What can we say about Eve (who we are only used to mentioning as the cause of humanity's first act of disobedience)?

In this literary work, we can see her as the woman who, despite her disobedience, stood up and built her life on the constant search for a promise given by God, which inspired her every day to **"KEEP PRODUCING."**

To stop seeing Leah as the unwanted wife, despised, and forgotten by Jacob, her husband, who spends much of her life trying to be considered by her own forces and then see her focus on praising the one who "her blessing comes from, whose name is Jehovah."

It is impressive to perceive a nomadic woman, with no trajectory like Jael, making use of "what she had at home, as a weapon of war to defeat the enemy, attacking him directly in the head."

Someone like Ruth, who we only saw as the daughter-in-law, and upon leaving Moab, she shines for her fidelity to Naomi. And then, we focus on her as a great reference to close the fatal doors of the past and extend towards a glorious future. We do not need to stand on our ground or lean on a non-existent lineage but give way to what God wants to do with us. See the Shunammite woman keeping her focus in the middle of a crisis. Or Bathsheba, accepting God's will, focused on her next level, and closed with a grand finale. Such an extraordinary work makes a majestic, focused objective and biblical defense of women's ministry, which could not be better.

In short, there are so many examples that the author gives us for reflection. Examples to understand that it does not matter if you are a simple woman condemned for your fault, a despised foreigner in a city with no apparent opportunity for development, or perhaps one who is only involved in a work routine.

NONE OF THIS IS ENOUGH FOR YOU TO LOSE YOUR ESSENCE. God will NEVER forget you. He did not create you to leave you, forgotten in the middle of the road. Now is when another level of your story really begins. Do not underestimate your present and start the journey through these pages that will lead you to find TREASURES IN THE ABYSS.

GO FORWARD!!! "WOMAN, REPSITION YOURSELF."

— **Bishop Vladimir Moore**

Introduction

One of the laws of Hermeneutics, which is the art of interpreting texts, especially those related to the sacred scriptures, establishes that the first time something is mentioned in the Bible, it marks the course of action of that something. Based on this, it is interesting to consider how the Bible first mentions the woman and the serpent that symbolizes Satan, and it establishes an eternal enmity between both creatures (See Genesis 3:15). Therefore, since ancient times, women have been the "target of attack" of the adversary, who continually works to make them victims of oppression, rejection, mistreatment, and abuse. But this is also why Satan has taken crushing losses when women like Maria W. Etter, Kathryn J. Kuhlman, Aimee McPherson, and many others have prioritized conquering the destiny for which they were designed and have accepted the challenge of revealing what they were created to do.

But many of these women have already fulfilled their specific assignment, and their mission on Earth has end-

15

ed. However, God's plans are still alive. Therefore, for each particular time and place, He has established the birth of previously appointed persons to carry out His plans.

In fact, the person who is now reading these lines is one of them, and Satan knows it. Therefore, he attacks you as he does, using everyone he finds as puppets of his property. His favorite instruments are the people closest to you because he knows the emotional fragility the female gender has. He knows the effect that betrayal, rejection, or any other type of mistreatment can produce to you, their eternal enemy.

Another strategy the adversary uses against the female gender is making women consider themselves victims. He makes women think they cannot recover from any situation that has happened to them in their past.

That is why he uses external elements to attack women and sends direct influences on their own emotions to make them feel stagnant, bitter, depressed, and rejected.

WOMAN, REPOSITION YOURSELF

He makes them believe there will never be a change in the situation they face and that the only way out they have is to flee or simply resign themselves to it. This certainly does not represent their destination, but only a specific time and circumstance, and God is allowing them to go through it to teach them something they will need to know for the next level.

But what is the cause of so much fury? The reason is simple: Satan knows what his enemies carry. He fears the thought of what could happen if the woman who is now reading this book responded as her Creator expects her to respond to the various challenges and attacks that she must continually face, rather than reacting how he expects her to.

However, you may be thinking, 'but how am I supposed to respond, and how should I face the various attacks that the enemy throws at me? We have obeyed the mandate given to us by the Lord to write this book, for which we have prayed that it may serve you as a tool of strength and guidance. Precisely to help you understand this as you advance towards the complete manifestation of the design with which you were created and fulfill the assignment for which you were appointed.

"For the earnest expectation of the creation eagerly waits for the revealing of the sons of God." **Romans 8:19 (NKJV).**

Are you ready? **Let us get started!**

Eve

Know your essence and keep producing

E ve was the first woman created by God, and there is much to appreciate about her life. Her creation reveals to us that everything the Lord does, He does with a sense of purpose to fulfill a specific purpose, and not just to occupy a place in space, as the following passage confirms:

"And the Lord God said, "It is not good that man should be alone; I will make him a helper comparable to him."
Genesis 2:18 (NKJV).

Based on this, we notice that before creating women, God observed that there was a need: **"It is not good for man to be alone,"** and for this need to be met, He elaborated an answer: **«I will make a helpmeet for him.»**

In other words, according to God's plan, the reason for Eve's existence was to serve as a complement and support to the man He had created. Still, since she is the first woman made, we cannot see her as an individual being, but more like the carrier of the essence the rest of the female gender would carry.

So, the same way Adam is the first man created and his design multiplies through the whole male gender, the creation of Eve brings with it the "base" design of the female gender, which would be impregnated in all the other women who would be born after her.

Now, God, in His omniscience, made each creature with a unique and specific design so that it can give full compliance to the assignment He gave. Therefore, when we speak about women's design, we refer to the form that was given to her to fulfill the mission for which she was created. Based on this, let us observe the following:

- *And God said: It is not good for man to be alone...* (Appreciation of need).

- *Therefore, I will make a helpmeet for him...* (assignment description).

Let us dive a little deeper into the terms "will" and "helpmeet." According to Hebrew (the language in which this text was initially written), the term "asa" means "I will" and is translated as: Designate, assign, dictate and edify. While the word "help" is "ezer" and is translated as: "Power or force that can save." The term "I will" appears twenty-one times in the Old Testament and refers to God when he is busy in activities of aid, relief, consolation, or redemption for his people, as in the case of the following passages: Exodus 18: 4, Deuteronomy 33: 7, Psalms 33:20, among others.

When considering this, we can confirm once again that God's intention when creating Eve was that she should serve as a help and support for Adam; but Satan's plan was that she should serve as a stumbling block and a channel of death. From the beginning of time, our adversary has had the purpose of stealing the essence of what God creates, and his first victim is the woman.

On the other hand, we cannot ignore the fact that, in the beginning, man's relationship with God was so close that Satan did not find a way to enter directly through him, but to get close, he used as a bridge the closest thing he had, which was the woman. Today, in general, turns out to be the other way around; Satan uses many men as a bridge to affect women whom the darkness cannot easily access because of their level of connection with the Creator.

But why was the tree of the knowledge of good and evil in the garden if God knew that his creation would disobey him if He put it there?

The answer is this: Because having the opportunity to disobey and not doing so is what proves how genuine our obedience is. In other words, we cannot say that we have authentically obeyed God until we have decided not to do so when having the opportunity to disobey.

The Lord will always allow something in front of us to test our obedience. The adversary also strategically uses this to make us disobedient, take away our position, and lead us to destruction. What is fully exposed in the way he deceived Eve.

Now, when we consider the details of the subtle trap used by the enemy to deceive the woman, we see that it contained the same tactics that he uses to deceive us as well. Take a look:

The opportunity to disobey and not do it demonstrate how genuine our obedience is.

HE IDENTIFIED A DESIRE: The desires that the enemy identifies within us can be diverse, such as the desire to have something or be with someone, carry out an act of revenge, or manipulate others. It may even be a legitimate desire, such as receiving something that is supposed to be given to us, but we are not receiving it for some reason.

The temptation begins when Satan suggests you give in through thought and fulfill a legitimate and evil desire in the wrong way or at the wrong time because according to his suggestions:

"You deserve it. Nothing will happen to you. You will feel better, you must have it now. You will not be the only one to fail the Lord ».

So, the temptation does not start outside of us but within us.

"For from the heart come evil thoughts, murder, adultery, all sexual immorality, theft, lying, and slander." **Matthew 15:19 (NLT)**

"But each person is tempted when he is lured and enticed by his own desire." **James 1:14 (ESV).**

HE USED A MEDIUM: Just as God uses people and things to bless us, Satan uses the same tools to destroy us. He does not show himself to us as he is but hides his true identity behind that in which he has found the qualities indicated to do so, which is evident in the following passage:

"<u>Now the serpent was more cunning</u> than any animal of the field which the Lord God had made." **Genesis 3: 1 (NASB).**

If we look up the word "cunning" in the dictionary, we find that it is defined as having or showing skill in achieving one's ends by deceit or evasion. So, it's not a coincidence that the bridge used by the adversary to reach the woman was the serpent because there is nothing that serves the devil and his interests more than an unconsecrated cunning.

In the same way, the means used by the enemy to reach you are not coincidental but subtly selected to increase the potentiality of the attack that he has been allowed to launch against you. We cannot fail to emphasize this because Satan can do nothing if he does not have the Lord's authorization to do so.

Now, God is beyond the reach of evil and does not urge anyone to fall into it. Still, He allows us to be tempted according to the capacity He has given us to reject the offers that the adversary puts before us. In other words, the Lord will never allow a temptation greater than our ability to withstand to come upon us.

"Let no one say when he is tempted, "I am being tempted by God," for God cannot be tempted with evil, and he himself tempts no one." **James 1:13 (ESV)**

"No temptation has overtaken you except what is common to mankind. And God is faithful; <u>he will not let you be tempted beyond what you can bear.</u> But when you are tempted, he will also provide a way out so that you can endure it." 1 **Corinthians 10:13 (NIV).**

Anyone who hopes to avoid the consequences of eating from the "forbidden fruit" should not approach the "tree" that produces it.

HE WAITED FOR HER TO BE ALONE: There are many temptations to which solitude lends great advantage because many, like Eve, in their moments of solitude tend to consider the tempter's proposal to approach what for them is "a forbidden tree." For this reason, we should use our solitude moments to strengthen and solidify our communion with the Lord and not to allow our unsanctified thoughts and desires to take the reins during that time. Anyone who hopes to avoid the consequences of eating the "forbidden fruit" should not approach the "tree" that produces it, as the Word of God exhorts us.

"Run from anything that stimulates youthful lusts. Instead, pursue righteous living, faithfulness, love, and peace. Enjoy the companionship of those who call on the Lord with pure hearts." **2 Timothy 2:22 (NLT).**

"And now, dear brothers and sisters, one final thing. Fix your thoughts on what is true, and honorable, and right, and pure, and lovely, and admirable. Think about things that are excellent and worthy of praise." **Philippians 4: 8 (NLT).**

Diverting our attention from what urges us to do the wrong thing is one of the most effective ways to overcome temptation.

HE SOUGHT A CONVERSATION OF INTEREST TO HER: It is wise, not only to observe the fruit of a problem but also to consider the root of it, and in this case, it is clear that the conversation between the woman and the serpent brought as a consequence the subtle dragging of the woman by Satan, to the ground that he wanted to take her to.

When the sage's reserves run out, no matter how much the tree wants to resist, its dryness will become evident.

The Bible calls our adversary "the father of all lies" because he cannot speak the truth. That is why whenever you give him an ear, he will always wrap you up to make you doubt what God has said about sin, leading you to consider things like these: Is it true that this is bad? Or does the Lord not want me to be happy?

While at other times, their arguments will be these: "Enjoy the moment, because God will understand you. He knows you are human; you will not be the first to fail Him".

Every alibi of the enemy will always contain a falsehood or simply a half-truth, just as we can appreciate in the following text:

The Lord will never allow a temptation greater than our capacity to support to come upon us.

"The serpent was the shrewdest of all the wild animals the Lord God had made. One day he asked the woman, "Did God really say you must not eat the fruit from any of the trees in the garden?" "Of course, we may eat fruit from the trees in the garden," the woman replied. 3 "It's only the fruit from the tree in the middle of the garden that we are not allowed to eat. God said, 'You must not eat it or even touch it; if you do, you will die.'" "You won't die!" the serpent replied to the woman." **(Genesis 3:1-4)**

Anyone who hopes to avoid the consequences of eating from the "forbidden fruit" should not approach the "tree" that produces it

---

Now, it is possible that some reading this passage may say to themselves: "But the man and the woman did not die at the moment they ate from the tree," and it is true, at that precise moment, they did not die. But because of their disobedience, they ingested death. Although they were still alive after eating the fruit that God had told them not to eat, death had entered them, and its manifestation (although not instantaneous) would undoubtedly be imminent.

To explain this better, we will use the following illustration: When a tree is pulled out of the ground, its leaves do not lose their greenness immediately. There are cases where it can take up to three weeks for the leaves to dry out, and some people may say, "They cut this tree down, but its leaves are still green! However, the greenness exhibited by the leaves of a tree after it has been cut is due to the sap it absorbed through the root while it was connected to the ground, which upon receiving the root, it carried to the trunk, and the trunk passed on to the branches for the branches to pass on to the leaves. But when the root is detached from the ground, it no longer receives the sap that it previously carried to the trunk, and once the trunk runs out of sap reserves, it cannot carry life to the branches, and the

When the sage's reserves run out, no matter how much the tree wants to resist, its dryness will become evident.

branches, not being able to receive life from the trunk, cannot transmit it to the leaves either. Therefore, when the sap reserves run out, no matter how much the tree wants to resist, its dryness will become evident.

The same happened with Adam and Eve. Sin had disconnected them from their communion with the Lord, similar to trees' connection with the ground through their roots. Because *"...the wage of sin is death..."* **Romans 6:23 (ESV)**. And it is precisely destruction and death that Satan seeks to bring into our lives, with the continuous and diverse incitements to sin that he makes to us.

Now, Adam and Eve disobeyed and were judged, but God, in his just judgment, was not going to leave the others involved without a sentence. So, the punishment of judgment was issued for the serpent, for being the instrument used to execute the deception, and the sentence of judgment was given for Satan, for being the intellectual author of the deception.

«*The Lord God said to the serpent, "Because you have done this, cursed are you above all livestock and above all beasts of the field; on your belly you shall go, and dust you shall eat all the days of your life.* » **Genesis 3:14 (ESV)**

«*I will put enmity between you and the woman, and between your offspring and her offspring; he shall bruise your head, and you shall bruise his heel*» **Genesis 3:15 (ESV)**.

The Lord will never allow a temptation greater than our capacity to support to come upon us.

The term "curse" used in verse fourteen, according to the Hebrew language, is "arar" and is translated as "To abominate and despise severely." Therefore, the curse issued by God against the serpent implied that it was going to be seen as a vile, abominable, and despicable creature while it existed.

In addition to this, we must emphasize the following statement: "You shall crawl." Precisely because of the position assigned to the serpent, the wound caused by the serpent to the woman's seed would be in the heel of the foot. At the same time, the seed that would come out of the woman would destroy her head. In other words, each one wounds from the level at which he is.

At this point, we must emphasize that although our struggle is certainly not with flesh and blood but spiritual (See Romans 6:12), God, in His perfect justice, also brings judgment on the flesh that allows itself to be used.

«… And you will eat the dust off the ground». Satan used the serpent to tempt Eve to eat what she should not, and therefore, she was sentenced by God to eat that which she did not want to eat for the rest of her life. So, while it is true that we must watch out for the attacks that may come to us through everything that has the likeness of a serpent, it is no less true that we must deny the entrance to everything that the enemy wants to put in us, to carry out his destructive purposes.

"But I am afraid that just as Eve was deceived by the serpent's cunning, your minds may somehow be led astray from your sincere and pure devotion to Christ." **2 Corinthians 11: 3 (NIV).**

"But if you cause one of these little ones who trusts in me to fall into sin, it would be better for you to have a large mill-stone tied around your neck and be drowned in the depths of the sea." **Matthew 18: 6 (NLT).**

"And I will cause hostility between you and the woman, and between your offspring and her offspring. He will strike your head, and you will strike his heel."». **Genesis 3:15 (NLT).**

The verb "will cause" used in this passage according to the Hebrew language is "shiit" and is translated as: "To ma-chine, to place, to weave, to put in front." While the word «enmity» is «eiba» and is translated as: «Hostility, opposi-tion, antipathy and armed conflict. » Therefore, consider-ing both concepts from the original root of the language, we can appreciate that this part of the punishment was more towards Satan (who was hiding behind the serpent) than for the serpent itself.

Therefore, when making a paraphrase of the expres-sion: *«I will cause hostility between you and the woman...»* said by the Lord, we obtain the following: «I will oversee causing opposition, rejection, antipathy and an armed conflict between you and the woman. I will make you op-posing entities as long as you exist, so you continually con-front each other ».

"His offspring will crush your head, and you will bite the heel of his foot." This part of the text contains the first prophecy given by God about the overwhelming victory

that Jesus (as the promised seeding) was to have over the kingdom of Satan since, through his death on the cross, he would bring salvation to all humanity. So just as sin entered the world through a woman, so would her seeding bring redemption to the whole world.

However, it is necessary to clarify that this prophecy not only embodies an enmity between the seed of the serpent and the seed of the woman (where the first ends up being crushed and crumbled by the latter). It also establishes a direct enmity between the woman as "gender" and the serpent as "devil."

So, in Genesis 3:15, in addition to the prophecy of redemption through Jesus Christ, it also marks the origin of a feeling of intolerance, rejection, and eternal repugnance between Satan and all that represents him, as well as the woman and all that she produces.

Anyone who is not ruled by Jesus Christ is a perfect candidate to be a helpful instrument in the hands of Satan. Now, to operate on Earth, what is spiritual needs what is human. That is why God looks for people who let themselves be used to carry out his plans. Satan also seeks the same thing.

So it is always on the prowl, trying to find anyone who gives it access to damage and mark for evil the woman's life, even from childhood.

Everyone who is not governed by Jesus Christ is a perfect candidate to be an instrument in the hands of Satan, and everyone who allows himself to be used by him becomes a representative of his interests.

Have you ever wondered why women tend to contend with the same gender as intensely as they do? One of the reasons for this is that the adversary does not want to have two of his enemies united. In fact, he is afraid of the simple idea that one becomes all that it can be. That is why his concern increases even more when there is unity between two or more women who understand and strive to fulfill the purpose that the Lord has entrusted to them.

The only unions between females that Satan enjoys are those that represent his interests.

Therefore, it is very common to find an abundance of jealousy, contention, rivalry, and envy within the same gender.

WOMEN'S INSECURITY OFFERS AN ADVANTAGE TO THE ENEMY

The feeling of insecurity is one of the cracks most exploited by the adversary to make a woman rage against another. Because women who do not understand the grace they carry and the talents God has given them, seek to overshadow the grace and gifts that have been deposited in the lives of others.

Everyone who is not governed by Jesus Christ is a perfect candidate to be an instrument in the hands of Satan.

But when a woman recognizes her identity and understands her worth, she understands that she is unique and has no replacements, like each of the women God has created. So, there is no advantage or gain in competing, but in complementing one another, unifying in purpose so that together we can comply with God's ordinances and ruin the adversary's plans of destruction.

The only female unions that Satan enjoys are those that represent his interests. He loves to see women united to accomplish sinful ends, but he despises to see them united to fulfill the assignment for which they were created. What assignment? Revealing all that God created them to be and which the Maker of them re-established even though the adversary wanted to undo. Because, after the sentence of judgment had been passed upon all the participants in sin, including the woman, the story of history continues with the following: *"And Adam called his wife's name Eve because she was the mother of all living."* **Genesis 3:20.** Something that turns out to be interesting for the following reasons:

◆ **The meaning of her name:**

The Hebrew translation for Eve's name is "khavvá," which translates as: "giver of life and the first woman."

◆ **The moment when this name was given:**

At this point, it is helpful to remember that woman was created as God's response to man's need for companionship.

Therefore, her design and the Creator's essence equipped her to fulfill such an objective. In this same context, it is worth noting that before the fall, the woman's name was "woman" but before being taken out of the garden, during the crisis, Adam gave her the name "Eve," which as we have already seen is translated as "giver of life and the first woman." This shows that the woman kept the essence with which she had been created, even after failing.

Now, it is essential to point out that the woman's capacity to give life is not only limited to being able to gestate a human being in her womb and give birth to it after nine months. It also includes her capacity to give life to everything that enters her and everything she touches.

But in addition to "giver of life," the name Eve is translated as "first woman," which makes it clear that just as there was a "first woman," there will be later women. And this becomes even more interesting if we remember that the name in biblical terms refers to the essence and destiny of the person named. In other words, Eve, as the first woman, was designed to be a giver of life, but all women born after her possess this same essence and ability.

_____

The only unions between females that Satan enjoys are those that represent his interests

_____

Because of this, every woman born has a physical womb, but she also has an emotional "womb." She has a mental "womb" and a spiritual "womb." This is how her

34

design and essence allow her to give life in all its expression.

God gave the woman the faculty to receive things into her, nurture them, mature them, and give them back fully developed. In other words, whatever you give to a woman, she will potentiate it. As the British poet and novelist William Golding said, "The woman is an improver, and if she is willing to use her faculties, whatever you give her, she will take it to a higher level. If you give her a sperm, she will give you back a child; if you give her a house, she will give you a home; if you give her an idea, she will give you a project; if you give her food, she will give you back a meal; and if you give her a smile, she will give you her heart."

God will never put something in us, something that He does not intend to use. So, all the gifts, talents, and abilities that he has given us have been to fulfill the assignment that he has entrusted to us entirely.

So, if at any time you have asked yourself some of the following questions, God gave women the ability to receive things within her, nurture them, make them mature and then return them fully developed.

Here we provide you with what we hope will serve as an answer:

- ◆ Why does God let me be with such troubled people? **Answer**: Because you can help them become better than they are.

- ◆ Why did I get to have a family like the one I have? **Answer**: Because with the design you carry, you can work with them until they become a family that serves as a model for others.

- ◆ Why did I have to go through all that I have gone through in life? **Answer**: Because due to the essence that you carry, you can take the bad experiences that happen to you, recycle them, and turn them into testimonies that serve as a blessing, strength, and edification to the lives of others.

So, you are not a victim of what you experienced in the past, nor the circumstances you may be facing right now. Instead, you are a daughter of God and an enemy of Satan who made a terrible mistake by attacking you because your Maker prepared you to take the adverse situations you are exposed to as a stage to reveal the life-giver within you.

At this point, I want to re-emphasize that the sentence issued by God against the serpent makes it clear that his crushing blow would not come directly from the woman. Instead, it comes from her seed, which according to the Hebrew translation, is "zera," which means: «fruit, descendant, to be fertile. » And although (as we already mentioned) this prophecy refers to the victory that Jesus would have over Satan,

God gave the woman the faculty to receive things into her, nurture them, mature them, and give them back fully developed.

36

it also reveals why the enemy fears everything that women (as his sworn enemy) can produce when she puts it in the hands of God. For this reason, to obstruct his productivity, the adversary always seeks to carry out one of these three actions:

Your Maker prepared you to take the adverse situations you are exposed to as a stage to reveal the life-giver within you.

1. Sterilize her, so she does not produce anything.

2. Urge her to misuse what she produces.

3. Take the life out of her production.

The last one was precisely what he wanted to do with Eve, but to understand it better, let us return to observe what the Lord said to the serpent about the woman's seeding: *«He will strike your head, and you will strike his heel. »* **Genesis 3:15b (NIV).**

In this part, we cannot overlook the fact that having been in heaven as part of the angelic army of the Creator (See Ezekiel 28:12-16), Satan knew the character and steadfastness of the Lord. He did not doubt that having come from the mouth of God, his defeat by the seed of the woman would unfailingly occur. But even knowing this, he was unwilling to let it happen without doing all he could to try to prevent it.

So, from the very moment the sentence was passed, he kept a close eye on what was coming out of the woman's womb to harm him. So, he paid particular attention to Cain, her first son, thinking that this could have been the seeding he had been warned about.

However, when we see the name that Eve gave to Cain, whose translation is "acquisition," and consider what she expressed at the time of giving birth, we can deduce that she could also think that this could have been the seed in which the promise was to be fulfilled.

«... *When she gave birth to Cain, she said, "With the Lord's help, I have produced a man!* **Genesis 4: 1 (NIV).**

And this is what also happens to many people when they receive a promise from God. Thinking that the fulfillment of the promise will be immediate, they make decisions and carry out actions that, although they are not wrong, are carried out at the wrong time. Because although everything God indeed says He does, it is no less true that the fulfillment of what He tells us always takes more time than we think.

That was what happened to Eve, to whom the Lord was certainly to give the seeding who would crush the serpent's head, but this was not immediately fulfilled. However, although Eve did not see what she expected in her first seed, she kept on producing instead of stopping.

How about you? What do you do when things do not turn out as you expected? What is your reaction when after doing everything right for you and having obeyed in all that you should, you see a different result than the one the Lord told you you would see?

I ask God that no matter how you have reacted up to now, from now on, take as a reference for action the legacy that Eve left us, and whatever happens and whatever you see, always decide to **KEEP PRODUCING!**

"Later she gave birth to his brother and named him Abel." **(See verse 4: 2).**

Abel, whose name means «that which ascends or vapor,» was the second son of Eve. So, when she gave birth to him, she could have thought that the prophecy given to her could be manifested through her second son (since the birth of her first child was not fulfilled). But it was not like that.

Instead, the first seed, Cain, allowed Satan to destroy all the seeds of his enemy, to fill his heart with apathy, rebellion, jealousy, and envy. Consequently, he ended up killing his brother Abel, the second seed of the woman. Let us see what the Bible tells us about it:

It is no less true that the fulfillment of what He tells us always takes more time than we think.

"When it was time for the harvest, Cain presented some of his crops as a gift to the Lord. Abel also brought a gift—the best portions of the firstborn lambs from his flock. The Lord accepted Abel and his gift, but he did not accept Cain and his gift. This made Cain very angry, and he looked dejected.

"Why are you so angry?" the Lord asked Cain. "Why do you look so dejected? You will be accepted if you do what is right. But if you refuse to do what is right, then watch out! Sin is crouching at the door, eager to control you. But you must subdue it and be its master."

One day Cain suggested to his brother, "Let's go out into the fields." And while they were in the field, Cain attacked his brother, Abel, and killed him. Afterward the Lord asked Cain, "Where is your brother? Where is Abel?" "I don't know," Cain responded. "Am I my brother's guardian?" But the Lord said, "What have you done? Listen! Your brother's blood cries out to me from the ground! Now you are cursed and banished from the ground, which has swallowed your brother's blood. No longer will the ground yield good crops for you, no matter how hard you work! From now on you will be a homeless wanderer on the earth."* **Genesis 4: 3-12 (NLT).**

In the text we just saw, it is revealed that here too, Satan makes his presence felt (although this time it is more discreetly than in his previous intervention) and succeeds in dragging Cain into his web of sin by making use of the following plan of action:

1. He identified a door for his entrance: The entrance of the adversary into Cain's life was the feeling of anger that he had because God was pleased with the offering that his brother Abel presented to him.

Time passed, and one day Cain brought an offering of the produce of his harvest to the Lord. Also, Abel brought the first and best young of his sheep to the Lord. The Lord looked with pleasure at Abel and his offering, but he did not look at Cain or his offering that way, so Cain got very angry and made a very angry face. (Verse 7).

But over time, many people wondered: Why was God pleased with Abel's offering and not with Cain's?

The answer to this is based on the following: Cain brought "some of his crops" while Abel brought "the best portions of the firstborn lambs from his flock." In other words, Cain's offering was based on "fulfilling what he owed," but Abel's offering was based on "giving God the best of what he had." Therefore, even the New Testament writings bear witness to it, saying: *"It was by faith that Abel brought a more acceptable offering to God than Cain did. Abel's offering gave evidence that he was a righteous man, and God showed his approval of his gifts. Although Abel is long dead, he still speaks to us by his example of faith."* **Hebrews 11: 4 (NLT)**

So, the biblical reality about this is not that God favored Abel; it was that Abel favored God over his possessions, and those who choose to give the Lord their best will always be rewarded according to their level of commitment. Cain, however, was the type of person who does things with

It is no less true that the fulfillment of what He tells us always takes more time than we think.

mediocrity and expects to receive the same reward as those who do their best and do things with excellence.

At this point, however, some may be thinking:

But why was God not pleased with Cain's offering if it was also a gift? To get an answer to this, we must remember that we do not give to God; We give back to God from what He gives us because He is the owner of everything that exists, while we are only stewards of what He puts in our hands.

In fact, when the Bible speaks to us about how we are to offer to the Lord, it says to bring or return to Him from what we have previously received from Him. Let us look at just a few of the biblical passages that prove this:

- ♦ *«But who am I, and who are my people, so that we can give something to you? Everything we have has come from you, and we bring to you only what you first gave us!»* **1 Chronicles 29:14 (NLT).**

- ♦ *"...bring the best of the first fruits of your land to the house of the Lord your God."* **Exodus 23:19 (NASB).**

- ♦ *"Bring the whole tithe for the funds of the temple, and then there will be food in my house."* **Malachi 3:10 (NIV).**

- *"... Give to Caesar what belongs to Caesar and give to God what belongs to God." ***Mark 12:17 (NLT)**.

Now let us continue with the evaluation of the plan of action used by the adversary to cause Eve's first seed to sin:

2. He urged Cain not only to be filled with zeal and envy against his brother but also to kill him.

Therefore, the Lord warns him: «*You will be accepted if you do the right thing, but if you refuse to do the right thing, then be very careful! Because sin is at the door, lurking and eager to control you; but you must dominate it and be its master* ». **Genesis 4: 7 (NLT)**.

When we consider this passage carefully, we can observe several interesting points such as the following:

You will be accepted if you do what is right... In saying these words to Cain, the Lord expresses to him: If you do right from now on and repent of your sin, you will be able to bring reformation to your heart. Your life will be aligned, your sacrifice will be accepted, and your honor restored.

But if you refuse to do what is right, then be careful!... If you do not decide to do right and instead of humbling yourself, you choose to persist in the wrong attitude, then be careful...

Because sin is at the door, lurking and eager to control you... In this part, the Lord makes it clear to Cain that due to his angry attitude, sin (referring specifically to the act of murder which, by disobeying God's warning, he ends up committing later on) stood at the door like a wild beast, and it was anxiously waiting to be given access to attack and dominate him.

But you must dominate it and be its master... This part of the statement certifies the following truth: we become the authority of what we decide to defeat, but what we are not willing to overcome becomes our authority.

God will never ask us to do anything He has not enabled us to do. So, by telling Cain that he was to dominate and be the master of the sin that sought to dominate him, the Lord is making it clear to him: *Cain, you just need to make the decision and be ready to beat it because you can certainly do it.* But, instead of dominating sin, Cain allowed himself to be carried away by it, obeying like a slave to the incitement that Satan did to him to assassinate his brother Abel, which (like every suggestion of the adversary) brought him such terrible consequences.

"...Then He said, "What have you done? The voice of your brother's blood is crying out to Me from the ground. Now you are cursed from the ground, which has opened its mouth to receive your brother's blood from your hand. When you cultivate the ground, it will no longer yield its strength to you; you will be a wanderer and a drifter on

We do not give to God; We give back to God from what He gives us.

44

EVE

the earth." Cain said to the Lord, "My punishment is too great to endure!" **Genesis 4: 10-13 (NASB).**

In this part, it is helpful to remember that the name of Abel means: "That which ascends or vapor" so that even after death, his essence ascended to God, claiming justice and the Lord showed justice.

So, as we have seen, in the first seed of Eve, which was Cain, the promise that had been given to him was not

> *God will never ask us to do anything He has not enabled us to do.*

fulfilled, but this promise was not fulfilled in Abel, his second seed, because his brother Cain killed him. Nevertheless, far from stopping because of this, Eve steadfastly kept producing and gave birth to her third son.

«*And Adam knew his wife again, and she bore a son and called his name Seth, for she said, "God has appointed for me another offspring instead of Abel, for Cain killed him."* » **Genesis 4:25 (ESV).**

According to the Hebrew language, the name Seth is translated as: «put in place of» because in place of Abel, Eve was given Seth, so that from his offspring would come forth the seed of the one to whom she had been given by promise, who would crush the head of the adversary.

This is also what the Lord does with us. Despite not immediately seeing what He said He would give us; we continue to believe in Him. Despite seeing what we understood as God's gift to us die, we do not give up. Despite our pain, brokenness, disappointment, and uncertainty, we continue to walk, advance, and continue to produce.

"So, _let's not get tired_ of doing what is good. _At just the right time_ we will reap a harvest of blessing if we don't give up." **Galatians 6: 9 (NLT).**

Chapter Principles

1. Everything the Lord does, He does with a sense of intention to fulfill a specific purpose, and not just to occupy a place in space.

2. We cannot say that we have obeyed God authentically, until we have had the opportunity to disobey him, but we have decided not to do so.

3. Just as God uses people and things to bless us, Satan uses the same tools to destroy us.

4. Satan cannot do anything if he does not have the Lord's permission to do it.

5. Diverting our attention from what urges us to do the wrong thing is one of the most effective ways to overcome temptation.

6. Our moments of solitude should be used to strengthen our communion with the Lord and not allow our unsanctified thoughts and desires to take control of that time.

7. Every alibi of the enemy will always contain a falsehood or simply a half-truth.

8. Although our struggle is certainly not with

flesh and blood but spiritual, God in His perfect justice also brings judgment on the flesh that allows itself to be used.

9. To operate on Earth, what is spiritual needs what is human; therefore, to carry out his plans, God looks for people who allow themselves to be used. To carry out his plans, Satan also looks for the same.

10. Women who do not understand the grace they carry, and the talents God has given them, generally seek to overshadow the grace and gifts that have been deposited in the lives of others.

11. A woman's capacity to give life is not only limited to being able to gestate a human inside her womb and give birth to it at nine months, but also encompasses her capacity to give life to everything that enters her and everything she touches.

12. God will never put anything in us that He does not intend to use. So, all the gifts, talents, and abilities He has given us have enabled us to fulfill the assignment He has given us.

13. Satan knew the character and steadfastness of the Lord and did not doubt that coming from the mouth of God, his defeat by the seed of the woman would inevitably occur.

14. Those who decide to give the Lord their best will always be rewarded according to their level of dedication.

15. We become the authority of what we decide to conquer, but that which we do not choose to overcome becomes our authority.

Leah

Rewarded for Being Underappreciated

The second woman we will consider in this book is Lea, whose name comes from the Hebrew root "laa," which translates to "tired, exhausted, or weary." Leah was the wife of Jacob, who did not love her. Jacob was Abraham's grandson and Isaac's son, whose personality was revealed even before he was born.

Jacob's mother was Rebekah, who consulted the Lord about why it was hard for her to get pregnant. She wanted an answer about why this was happening to her, and the Lord replied: «*Two nations are in your womb, two peoples shall be separated from your body; one people shall be stronger than the other, <u>and the older shall serve the younger</u>*» **Genesis 25:23 (NKJV).**

When Rebekah gave birth to the twins, Esau, Jacob's brother, came out of the womb first, but Jacob's hand came out as an extension of him, grabbing him by the heel. Hence the name Jacob means "he who takes by the heel, he who supplants, or he who wants to occupy a position that does not belong to him." However, the primogeniture had been assigned by God to Jacob before he was born, but the fact of using human movements (even from his mother's womb) to obtain it was why he was given that name.

There is great danger in becoming anxious when we certainly have a promise from the Lord, but the time of its fulfillment has not yet come. Because when anxiety takes over, we allow ourselves to be dragged by it to do things that, according to our own perception, will contribute to the acceleration of the fulfillment of what the Lord has told us. But perception influenced by despair will never be a good counselor.

When God's time for something to happen has not yet arrived, by manipulating people and things, we will only succeed in producing chaos, disasters, and sometimes even delays in what the Lord has said He would do in due time.

God does not need us to manipulate anything for what He promised to do to be accomplished. When the sky clock strikes the appointed time for the fulfillment of something, nothing on Earth that tries to oppose Him will be able to stop Him.

Perception influenced by despair will never be a good counselor.

"Whatever the Lord pleases He does, in heaven and in earth, in the seas and in all deep places." **Psalm 135:6 (NKJV).**

Now, to better appreciate the plot of the event in Jacob's life, let us look at the following verses:

> *But perception influenced by despair will never be a good counselor.*

"It happened that when Isaac grew old, and his eyes grew dark, and he was blind, he called Esau his eldest son and said to him: My son. And he answered: Here I am. And he said: Here I am already old; I do not know the day of my death.

Then Rebekah spoke to her son Jacob, saying: Behold, I have heard your father talking with Esau your brother, saying: Bring me game and make me a stew, so that I may eat, and bless you in the presence of the Lord before I die. Now, therefore, my son, obey my voice in what I command you. Now go to the cattle, and bring me two good goats from there, and I will make food for your father out of them, just as he likes; and you will take them to your father, and he will eat, so that he will bless you before his death."

"Now it came to pass, when Isaac was old and his eyes were so dim that he could not see, that he called Esau his older son and said to him, "My son." And he answered him, "Here I am." Then he said, "Behold now, I am old. I do not know the day of my death. So, Rebekah spoke to Jacob her son, saying, "Indeed I heard your father speak to Esau your brother, saying, 'Bring me game and make savory food for

WOMAN REPOSITION YOURSELF

me, that I may eat it and bless you in the presence of the Lord before my death.' Now therefore, my son, obey my voice according to what I command you. Go now to the flock and bring me from there two choice kids of the goats, and I will make savory food from them for your father, such as he loves. Then you shall take it to your father, that he may eat it, and that he may bless you before his death." So, he went to his father and said, "My father." And he said, "Here I am. Who are you, my son?" Jacob said to his father, "I am Esau your firstborn; I have done just as you told me; please arise, sit and eat of my game, that your soul may bless me." But Isaac said to his son, "How is it that you have found it so quickly, my son?" And he said, "Because the Lord your God brought it to me." Isaac said to Jacob, "Please come near, that I may feel you, my son, whether you are really my son Esau or not." So, Jacob went near to Isaac his father, and he felt him and said, "The voice is Jacob's voice, but the hands are the hands of Esau." And he did not recognize him, because his hands were hairy like his brother Esau's hands; so, he blessed him." **Genesis 27: 1-2, 6-10, 18-23 (NKJV).**

This act of deception committed by Jacob, with the help of his mother Rebekah (although it contained a high level of sagacity), only succeeded in making him the cause of the disappointment and discontent of Isaac, his father. Also, the "target of attack" of the wrath of his brother Esau, cause for which he fled to the land of Haran, to the house of Laban, Rebekah's brother, with precise instructions to take a wife only from the daughters of that house.

While there, Jacob met Rachel, Laban's youngest daughter, whom the Bible describes as a woman of "fair countenance and beautiful looks," and fell madly in love with her. So, he agreed with Laban to work for seven long years to have her as his wife. But because of his great love for her, these years seemed like days. (See Genesis 29:18-20).

When the time of the agreement for Rachel to be given as a wife to Jacob was fulfilled, Laban summoned all the men of the place and prepared a feast that gave place to the long-awaited wedding night. But for that night, he, who was to become her father-in-law twice over, had prepared a trap for her, which indeed later led Jacob to remember the trap he had also set for his brother Esau. So instead of Laban giving him Rachel as his wife (as they had agreed), he gave him Leah, his eldest daughter, whom the Bible describes as a woman with "delicate" eyes. According to the Hebrew language, this term is "rac" and translates as: "weak or soft," which is why many commentators have come to believe that she may have suffered from what is medically known as strabismus. To which is added the problem of not being the woman that the man she had married longed to have as a wife.

On the other hand, it is easy to deduce that Leah felt inferior to her sister Rachel, from the very day of her birth, due to Rachel's physical beauty and Leah lacked (according to the biblical text).

And although her father had given her to Jacob as a wife, and on their wedding night she had received attention, affection, and love that she had never experienced before, Leah knew that Jacob's love did not really inspire this treatment for her, but for her sister Rachel.

Now, perhaps at this point, you are wondering: But how could Jacob not realize that he had been deceived? How could he not perceive that the one to whom he was giving himself that night was not Rachel but Leah? This happened because of the tradition that the bride had to enter the chamber (specially prepared for the wedding night) covered with a dark veil. She had to keep it on until the following day, when the marriage covenant was deemed to have been concluded with the act of removing the veil. But when morning came, when Jacob removed the veil from Lea's face, he was frustrated, hurt, and deceived, so he quickly went to confront Laban.

Here we can see confirmed what the sacred text clearly states: *"Do not be deceived: God cannot be mocked. A man reaps what he sows."* **Galatians 6: 7 (NIV).**

Because of this, we see here who once cheated, being cheated, and who once deceived, being deceived.

On the other hand, Leah was caught between the consequences of the manipulative and self-centered way in which her father had carried out this deception, and between the rejection that her husband (for having been deceived) manifested to her. In other words, Lea had not chosen to live through this, but even though she had not chosen it, this was a reality she had to face.

And you, have you ever had to live the consequences of the bad actions that others have done? Lea is a clear example of someone who has had to go through this.

Like that of every woman (or at least most of them), Leah's goal was to feel loved, admired, and respected for who she was, but instead, she felt used, unloved, and undervalued.

On the other hand, after Jacob had complained to Laban about what he had done to her, Laban made one more agreement with him: to also give Rachel his youngest daughter for his wife, if she would work for him for another seven years.

«*So, it came about in the morning that, behold, it was Leah! And he said to Laban, "What is this that you have done to me? Was it not for Rachel that I served with you? Why then have you deceived me?" But Laban said, "It is not the practice in our place to marry off the younger before the firstborn. <u>Complete the week of this one, and we will give you the other also for the service which you shall serve with me, for another seven years.</u>" Jacob did so and completed her week, and he gave him his daughter Rachel as his wife. So, Jacob had relations with Rachel also, and indeed he loved Rachel more than Leah, and he served with Laban for another seven years.* »* **Genesis 29: 25-28,30 (NASB)**.

So just one week after his wedding with Leah, Jacob became the husband of Rachel, the woman he loved and the one he yearned for to give him all his love, affection, warmth, and understanding. Can you imagine how all of this could have made Lea feel? Do you have any idea how this could have affected this woman's self-esteem?

Perhaps neither you nor I can fully understand it, but it certainly was not the same with the Lord's appreciation of it. This is revealed in the following verse:

"Now the Lord saw that Leah was unloved, and He opened her womb, but Rachel was unable to have children." **Genesis 29:31 (NIV).**

The term "saw" according to the Hebrew language is "raa" and is translated as: "attend, consider, contemplate, lift, estimate and acknowledge."

Therefore, Jacob's contempt for his wife Leah made the justice of the Lord manifest in her favor, attending her, considering her, contemplating her, lifting her, esteeming her, and recognizing her.

Oh, how much good certain painful experiences do us, even if at the time we live them, it does not seem that they can in any way favor us! Something that the Bible clearly shows us when it says:

"When the Lord saw that Jacob despised Leah, he granted her to have children." Making it clear that Jacob's contempt for Leah was what served as a trigger for God's grace and defense to manifest on her behalf. This proves that no matter

how underestimated or rejected you are, the people around you when you have the Lord's favor and grace on your side.

However, it is also interesting to consider Leah's attitude towards God's blessing. Since, instead of maintaining a humble and passive posture, she used the gift of productivity that the Lord had given her to try to get the man's attention. Something that we can appreciate in the following passages:

«*Leah conceived and gave birth to a son, and named him Reuben, for she said, "Because the Lord has seen my affliction; surely now my husband will love me."*» **Genesis 29:32 (NASB).**

She named her first child "Reuben" with the intention of being cared for and recognized. According to the Hebrew translation, Reuben means: "look at me or see a son." At this point, we want to re-emphasize that it is not wrong to want to be appreciated, valued, and recognized, but to exhibit what we have to attract the attention of others, is not the purpose for which God's gifts have been given to us, and whenever they are used for this purpose, we cannot produce with them the real results for which those gifts were given to us.

Leah thought that the birth of Reuben would put an end to Jacob's attention to Rachel, which is revealed in the following expression: «*Surely now my husband will love me.* » **Genesis 29: 32b (NASB).**

But Jacob did not love her.

Leah was married to a man who, all day long, did not even bother to greet her or ask how she felt. Because, although Jacob saw her daily, he never bothered to look at her. He did not realize if she had gained or lost any weight. He did not notice if she was wearing a new outfit or pair of shoes, and he never noticed if she changed her hair or used the same hairstyle. Because for Jacob, Lea lived in the house but did not live in his world. And although she had given him a son and a "strategic" name to get his attention, this son did not result in her husband looking at her, much less succeeding in making him love her.

At this point, we should note that the rejection of any woman by the people she loves is usually one of the weapons most used by Satan to affect her emotions, and when this woman does not face the situation as it should, it can even affect her spiritual and physical self. After a while, she begins to consider as valid the whispers that the adversary makes to her in such a situation, such as these: "The reason you are rejected is because you do not have any value," "You do not have the ability to be the person that others expect you to be "and that is where the rejected woman thinks: "I must do something to become what I am not yet." This is what Leah did when she named her first son "look at me," but when Jacob did not look at her as she expected, she proceeded to get pregnant once more and named her second child Simeon., whose translation is "Simeon" and means: "hear" or "hear me."

In her second attempt to get her husband's attention, Leah names the second child Simeon as if to say, "Okay Jacob, since you don't want to see me, then at least hear me." In this way, she wanted him to pay attention to her feelings, opinions, concerns, and emotions. She wanted to share with her husband how her day had been, what ideas she had produced, and what plans she would forge herself, but regardless of Leah's attempts to achieve this, her husband did not hear her.

One of the worst situations a woman can face is living with a man who ignores her. Unfortunately, there are many marriages where the woman does all the talking while the man ignores her. And this, of course, affects the couple's life, especially when the situation is not well managed by the person affected.

Every time Leah spoke the name of her son Simeon, she cried out to her husband, "Please listen to me." But Jacob would not listen to her.

So, in her stubborn persistence to get Jacob's attention, Leah became pregnant again and named her third son Levi, which translates as: "join me" or "connect with me," an act by which Leah desperately said to Jacob: "Connect with me. Can't you see that I am the one who is giving you

Oh, how much good certain painful experiences do us, even if at the time we live them, it does not seem that they can in any way favor us!

WOMAN REPOSITION YOURSELF

children? It is because of me that you have become a father. My sister is not giving you what I am giving you. Don't you realize that it is our relationship that God has blessed?".

At this point (as is obvious), we can observe that Jacob was fulfilling his marital duty to Leah, the cause for which she had given birth to all these children, but she still did not receive the affection she desired to have from her husband through this. Because loving someone is not the same as having sex with that someone, and I am sure that many of the women reading this know very well what I am referring to.

Leah's desire was not just to have sex with her husband. It was to be his close friend. It was to feel that she was close to him. She wanted Jacob to love her, to share with her the secrets of his life, and to express the desires of his heart. Leah really wished that their marriage was different with all her strength. Her longing was to be so united with Jacob that they would be "one" instead of two, as the Lord established when the marriage was founded.

"That is why a man leaves his father and mother and is united to his wife, and they become one flesh." **Genesis 2:24 (NIV).**

That was the relationship Leah desired to have with Jacob, from whom, despite having three sons and living with him under one roof, she felt distant and separated. So, by naming her third son: "join me" or "connect with me," Leah begged Jacob, saying: "Please join me and become one with me." But Jacob did not join.

In this story, we see that having children by a man does not guarantee a woman that he will look at her, listen to her or become one with her. Leah finally understood this truth, and the

The rejection of any woman by the people she loves is usually one of the weapons most used by Satan to affect her emotions

fact she did, made her take the correct position to face her situation, as she should have done from the beginning.

Because after several failed attempts, the same Leah we saw begging Jacob to pay attention to her, to love her, to take care of her and to value her, was the one who put an end to that chapter and with her head held high, she set out to open another one.

But what did Leah do this time? What was the new way she used to handle this affair?

Leah became pregnant for the fourth time, but her handling strategy would now be different because while she named her first son Reuben, which means "look at me," she named the second son Simeon, which means "listen to me," the third she called Levi, which means: "join me." When her fourth son was born, she named him Judah, which according to the Hebrew translation, is "Yehuda" and is translated as: "this time I will praise Jehovah."

By naming her fourth son "Judah," Leah was making the following clear and established: "With this son, a new sea-son begins in my life, where even though Jacob will not look at me, even though he will not listen to me, and even though he will not want to join me, I will stop worrying about what I cannot change, and focus on praising the source of my blessing, whose name is Jehovah.".

So, with her new attitude, Leah gives us an example of how we should respond to the different pressures that arise in our marriages; when we do not receive what we expect to receive from our husbands or when things at home do not end the way we worked for years for them to end.

Do not let yourself be overwhelmed. Put an end to particular chapters and praise Jehovah.

In addition to the above, do not think that everything has come to an end if your boss decides to give the promotion to someone else, instead of giving to you, even if you worked hard. Do not think that your life has no value when you feel that your father loves your sister more than he loves you, or if you see that your mother treats your brother with more affection than she shows you. Do not get discouraged when you see that nothing works after doing everything humanly possible to earn the affection and respect of a person. Do not give any of this the power to frustrate you or make your life bitter; just use Leah's strategy, put an end to those chapters and make the decision to praise Jehovah.

If you feel tired of being ignored or disrespected or have realized that certain people do not like you, it is time to close chapters with a new attitude. You need to state I do not need the attention of a human being to feel fulfilled, I do not need a man to listen to me to feel valued, and even if some do not want to join me, I will not stop feeling loved. Because I have realized that praise to my Creator can come from within me, that I have access to communicate with the source from which I came, and that by praising my God, I can feel loved, understood, and appreciated. Because His ear is attentive to my praise and His Holy Spirit has come to be "one" with me.

So, friend, who is reading this:

- If you find yourself ill and it seems that your illness has no cure… **Praise Jehovah.**

- When your family members or friends do not understand or accept your relationship with the Lord… Praise Jehovah.

- If you were abandoned by your husband and feel that sadness and loneliness weigh you down, remember God has promised that he will never leave you or forsake you. So, wipe away your tears, get off the floor, and… **Praise Jehovah.**

- If you are a single mother and have no one to help you raise your children… **Praise Jehovah.**

- If you worked many years in a company from which you were fired in the end… **Praise Jehovah.**

◆ If you do not have the money you need to meet the commitments you have to face, place your anxiety in the Lord and let Him take care of what you cannot and… **Praise Jehovah.**

◆ If you feel that you are advanced in age, and you still do not know the person with whom you will share your life, trust in the Lord's care for you, do not despair, and while you wait… **Praise the Lord.**

This is because you will experience a significant discharge and liberation whenever you decide to connect with God and worship Him with all your strength. For the more you connect with the eternal, the less you worry about what is transient, and the deeper you deepen your relationship with the Lord, the less dependent you will be on the attentions that men can give you.

Although everything externally is gray, the "Sun of Justice" (that is God) will always shine within you.

« *"But for you who fear my name, the Sun of Righteousness will rise with healing in his wings. And you will go free, leaping with joy like calves let out to pasture.* » **Malachi 4: 2 (NLT).**

Being intimate with the God who created you leads you to understand your true identity. The more you know God, the more you realize the great value you have for Him. That is why when Leah understood that she should change the way she was handling things, she named his son number four "Judah," instead of giving it a name similar to those of the first three sons; and it is from this son that comes the tribe of Judah, the most powerful of all the tribes of Israel. From this tribe came illustrious kings like David and Solomon, but the highest distinction of this tribe is that from it came the Messiah Jesus Christ, the Savior of the world.

So, I seriously want to suggest that, like Leah, you decide from this very moment to "make Judah be born of you" because until you make your life "a walking altar of praise," you will always need a human to entertain you.

And until you set your eyes on the Lord, you will be looking for ways to make men see you, listen to you, understand you, tell you the value you have, tell you if you look good, if what you did, you did well, and more like these. But when you turn your face to God and concentrate your life only on the Lord, you will feel fulfilled, and you will understand that you are much more than what many of the people around you have appreciated up to this moment.

On another note, it is not possible to praise the Lord and at the same time be concerned about your needs; it is not possible to be immersed in the presence of the Lord and at the same time be immersed in anxiety about what others may be talking about you. You cannot be disturbed by the things you cannot control while praising the Lord with all your heart. So, rest in God and praise Him. For He is our Lord, our Cornerstone, our Rock, and the one upon whom our stability must depend.

Never build what you are by putting a man as your foundation because if you do, your firmness will only last until that certain man decides to walk away, and when he walks away, your whole world (because it was built on that man) will collapse. Therefore, some people dare to say to others:

"If I leave your life, everything you are falls apart" because they think they are those people's foundation instead of the Lord.

The rejection of any woman by the people she loves is usually one of the weapons most used by Satan to affect her emotions

So, on this day I want you to be very clear about the following: the fact that someone has decided to leave you does not mean that your "world" must collapse, it simply means that you must establish your life on the proper foundation, which is Jesus Christ, because (unlike men) He will never leave your side, and He will always accompany you and sustain you.

«*Therefore, this is what the Sovereign Lord says: "Look! I am placing a foundation stone in Jerusalem, a firm and tested stone. It is a precious cornerstone that is safe to build on. Whoever believes need never be shaken.*» **Isaiah 28:16 (NLT).**

Chapter Principles

1. When God's time for something to happen has not yet arrived, manipulating people and things will only produce chaos, disasters, and sometimes even delays in what the Lord has said He will do in due time.

2. When the clock in heaven marks the appointed time for the fulfillment of something, nothing that tries to oppose it on Earth will be able to stop it.

3. Jacob's contempt for Leah served as the trigger for God's grace and defense on her behalf.

4. It does not matter how underestimated or rejected you are by the people around you when you have the favor and grace of the Lord on your side.

5. Having children by a man does not guarantee a woman that he will look at her, listen to her, or become one with her.

6. You will experience a great release and liberation whenever you decide to connect with God and worship Him with all your might.

7. The more you deepen your relationship with the Lord, the less dependent you will be on the attention that men can give you.

8. Being intimate with the God who created you leads you to understand your true identity.

9. When you turn your face to God and concentrate your life only on the Lord, you will feel fulfilled, and you will understand that you are much more than what many of the people around you have appreciated up to this moment.

10. Never build what you are by putting a man as your foundation because if you do, your firmness will only last until that particular man decides to walk away from you.

11. The fact that someone has decided to move away from you does not mean that your "world" must collapse, but that you must rebuild what you are, having Jesus Christ as your foundation.

Jael

Attack the problem directly in the head

T he story of Jael is part of an exciting story from the book of Judges. But, to establish the proper foundation, before the main teaching that we want to highlight from this story, we will begin by saying that the time the judges ruled was when the people of Israel lived before being ruled by kings. Period, in which (according to the Bible) the people did what they thought best (See Judges 17:6). Something that, of course, made them face the due consequences.

God had formed the nation of Israel so that He could show His glory to all the other nations through them. But the children of Israel forgot the covenant they had made with the Lord, and He delivered them into the hands of their enemies. However, when they cried out to God for deliverance amid their bondage, He always raised someone to lead a redemption campaign and defeat the enemy peoples. These people were called "judges," and among the most prominent of them, we see Gideon, Samson, and Jephthah, but in addition, we also find a woman named Deborah.

Her story is narrated to us in chapter 4 of the book of Judges, saying that after the death of judge Ehud, the children of Israel again did evil in the sight of the Lord. Because of this, God gave them over to the Canaanites, who had Jabin for their king, and as captain of their army, Sisera, a man with a strong hand, who with nine hundred chariots of iron under his command, had oppressed Israel for twenty years.

But after two decades of suffering under this oppressive government, the people cried out to God, asking him to liberate them. In response to this request, the Lord raised Deborah of the tribe of Ephraim as judge and prophetess. (See Judges 4:1-5).

According to the story context, at that time, the men of Israel were too fearful and unorganized for battle. Therefore, after receiving an order from God, Deborah called Barak and told him to summon the army of the tribes of Naphtali and Zebulon on Mount Tabor because God was going to give him the victory over the enemy's army. Barak agreed to go, but only if Deborah would go with him; so, she agreed to go, but, before doing so, she made an interesting prediction, which is too often overlooked by many readers and students of the Bible. Deborah predicted that God would deliver the victory of the battle through a woman because she was going with Barak.

«*Barak told her, "I will go, but only if you go with me."* *"Very well," she replied, "I will go with you. But you will receive no honor in this venture, for the Lord's victory over Sisera will be at the hands of a woman."* » **Judges 4: 8-9 (NLT).**

Deborah is one of the several women that the Bible points out as a prophetess, a rank that also includes: Mary, Aaron's sister, Isaiah's wife, Anna, Huldah, among others.

On the other hand, some women were not prophetesses, but God still guided them and helped them perform great deeds in favor of the people. This is the case of Jael, whose name in Hebrew is "ya'el" like the name of a type of mountain goat, which is characterized by surviving in dry and rocky terrain, which is so fast and very difficult to catch. However, it also has an impressive ability to move from one mountain to another without losing stability.

Now, throughout the Old Testament, we can see how God placed tools of faith in the hands of Israel's deliverers to help them defeat their enemies. In the case of Samson, it was the jawbone of a donkey (Judges 15:16), while Shamgar's weapon of war was an ox goad (Judges 3:31). For David, it was the stones he took from the stream (1 Sam. 17:40). For the mighty Eleazar, it was his sword (2 Samuel 23:10); for Moses, it was his rod (Exodus 4:17); and for Jael, the woman in this story, her two tools of war were a sledgehammer and a stake. For God had promised that he would give victory by the hand of a woman, and so he did.

"And the Lord routed Sisera and all his chariots and all his army with the edge of the sword before Barak; and Sisera alighted from his chariot and fled away on foot. But Barak pursued the chariots and the army as far as Harosheth Ha-goyim, and all the army of Sisera fell by the edge of the sword; not a man was left." **Judges 4: 15-16 (NKJV).**

Once Sisera saw his army destroyed, he escaped and fled to Jael's tent, believing that she would protect him from the pursuing Israelite troops. Jael was the wife of Heber the Kenite, and Sisera's decision to flee to this territory was based on a peace agreement with King Jabin and the Kenites (See Judges 4:17).

The Kenites were highly skilled blacksmiths, so Sisera could also deduce that by fleeing there, he would be guaranteed protection and care for as long as it took for him to recover and be able to reestablish his army again. So Sisera entered Jael's tent and asked her to hide him under a blanket. Then he asked her for water, and instead of water, she gave him milk to drink. After drinking, exhausted by the battle, he fell asleep, and it was then that Jael took the opportunity to take the stake and the mallet in her house (typical tools of the blacksmiths) to pierce with these, Sisara's temples. In this way, Jael used what she had in her house as a weapon of war to finish with the enemy.

At this point, it is worth noting that in ancient times, it was a shame and dishonor for a man (and his living descendants) to be killed by a woman. (See Judges 9:52-54).

Thus, was fulfilled what the Lord had spoken through Deborah, saying that He would deliver Sisera into the hands of a woman. And although many consider Jael's action as a vile act of treason

The rejection of any woman by the people she loves is usually one of the weapons most used by Satan to affect her emotions

and deceit, respecting the different opinions that other writers may have on the matter, we will limit ourselves to highlight the courage and decision of this woman to proceed to eliminate the enemy in the way she did.

Therefore, Deborah sings a song of gratitude, mentioning Jael as an instrument chosen by God to deliver victory to the people.

"In the days of Shamgar, son of Anath, In the days of Jael, the highways were deserted, and the travelers walked along the byways. Village life ceased, it ceased in Israel, until I, Deborah, arose, arose a mother in Israel. Most blessed among women is Jael, the wife of Heber the Kenite; blessed is she among women in tents. He asked for water, she gave milk; she brought out cream in a lordly bowl. She stretched her hand to the tent peg, her right hand to the workmen's hammer; she pounded Sisera, she pierced his head, she split and struck through his temple. At her feet he sank, he fell, he lay still; at her feet he sank, he fell; where he sank, there he fell dead." **Judges 5: 6-7, 24-27 (NKJV).**

From this time on, just as it happened with Rahab and Ruth (unknown women who, because of their actions, were taken out of anonymity) because of her deed, Jael went from being a simple anonymous woman to being a hero for all the people.

Jael's story leaves us with several lessons, among which are the following:

◆ **Her victory was not consistent with her trajectory:**

She was a nomadic woman, with nothing in her background to indicate that she would end the life of a skilled captain, highly trained in warfare as Sisera was. But God is an expert at taking the ordinary and the simple and turning it into something glorious. So, the fact that you feel you are just an ordinary person is what qualifies you to be used by the Lord in an extraordinary way.

◆ **She was aware of the character who had entered her house:**

Jael was aware of who Sisera was and decided not to waste the opportunity of having this enemy in her house, to take the tools she had and pierce his head. In the same way, whenever the Lord allows certain things to enter our territory, we must also take the tools we have to attack them directly in the head and thus free the other members of our house from the oppression that this evil can cause.

In fact, it is probable that you are facing things right now that have also attacked other members of your family, and

God has allowed them to come to you, not only to confront them but in the name of Jesus, to eliminate them by piercing their heads. As we said in the first chapter of this book: *"You become the authority of that which you overcome, but that which overcomes you becomes your authority."* Therefore, the fight truly ends when you win the battle. And precisely, for you to win it, the Lord has placed on you the anointing that rots yokes, breaks chains, and destroys iniquity from the very head.

"In your strength I can crush an army; with my God I can scale any wall." **Psalm 18:29 (NLT).**

♦ **He used the tools that were in her house:**

Many people expect to receive from the outside what they should get from inside, and to know if you are one of them, I invite you to make the following consideration:

Have you ever said to God something like this: "Lord, if you gave me money, I could do this or that"?

"If I lived somewhere else and not in this place, things would be different" or "If I had the right connections, I could carry out such and such a project."

If your answer is yes, do not worry because you are not the only one. There was a time when the person who wrote this book also told the Lord the same thing.

77

This happened when I had not yet become a writer. Although many people asked me to write, I needed to be totally convinced that this important facet of my ministry would have the absolute support of the Lord, as everything we had done for Him up to that time. And just in the year 2012, while I was going through a very challenging process in my life, I visited my mentor and spiritual father (who was also my bishop). I expressed to him that the situation I was going through seemed to be much more than what I understood I could bear. And I remember he went into a brief silence after hearing me speak and seeing me cry intensely because of the terrible ordeal I was going through. Then he said to me, "There is a preacher I want you to listen to, and I know that when you do, God will use her to speak to your heart during this process." When he told me this, I immediately felt a sense of expectation, mixed with the hope that God would indeed use this woman to speak to me despite how bad I was feeling.

So, I immediately asked him: "What is her name to look her up? Then, with a very slight smile, he answered me: "She is my favorite preacher, and you know her; she is sitting in front of me right now."

That was very unexpected for me, but I also confess that I have rarely felt so confronted in my life as I did at that moment. I felt as if God himself, through him, had said to me: "Now it will not only be enough to preach good messages, but you will have to demonstrate the authenticity of what you preach by applying those messages to your own life."

So, that same afternoon when I arrived home (although it may seem absurd), I began to listen to some of the messages that I had recorded, and it was as if the Lord had taken my mouth in advance to instruct me in what I should do later. For, in one of those messages, God, through my mouth, said: "When you receive a strike from darkness, strike back instead of letting that attack overcome you."

Today I thank and give all the glory to the Lord for leading me to this because having listened to that instruction truly made me feel committed to authenticating what it said, STRIKING BACK. However, I needed to know exactly what this would mean for me since, at that time, I was praying three hours a day, fasting twice a week, memorizing two verses a day. And above all, always seeking (as I do now) to live an upright and pleasing life before the Lord, giving testimony of Him in everything I did.

So, in prayer, I asked God how I should STRIKE BACK, and after several days in prayer, the Lord spoke to my heart and said, "I want you to use the pain you feel now as contractions to bring forth your first book. Write because I will back you up. That word amazingly activated my passion for writing, and I will never forget how many times while I was writing, tears would run down my face and fall on the computer board, but I kept writing anyway. And one night, I prayed to the Lord saying: "My God, please allow that, as many tears have been shed amid this process in which you have commanded me to write this book, so many testimonies will arise because of the word that you are directing me to write."

79

When I finished the writing of the book, the Lord told me: "Proceed with the preparation of the book and schedule the launching," something with which once again my faith was being tested, since the preparation of a book consists of: spelling correction, proofreading, layout, cover design, and printing, which when added together gave an amount of money that I lacked. But despite this, God's indication was: "Prepare the book and schedule the launching." So, I prayed again and said, "Lord, you know I don't even have the money to prepare the book, so why are you directing me to schedule a launch as well?". At that moment, God spoke to my heart and said, "Because when you release what you have, you receive what you lack."

This word gave me the firmness I needed to execute the mandate I had received. Based on it, I made the proper arrangements with the proofreader, the layout designer, the cover designer, and the printer, covering (with the few resources I had) only a part of the cost of the work to the first two. According to the word I had received from God, I would be able to pay the total cost of the cover design and printing on the day of the launch.

And now, as I write this, I confess that I am smiling. The promise of payment I made to those people was based on conviction by obeying God's word, rather than believing that the book's sale would produce an amount capable of covering all those debts on the day of the launch. Somehow on that day, the provision of heaven would come so that I would be able to meet all those payments.

When the big day arrived, both my work team and I were totally amazed to see the tremendous amount of people that stood in long lines from early afternoon to purchase "I CHALLENGE YOU TO GROW," our first book, which up to this day has blessed the lives of thousands of people around the world, and that a few years after being launched, became a "bestseller" something for which we give all the glory and recognition to the Lord.

So today, as Jael did, I encourage you to decide to use the tools you have in "your house" and dare to release what you have and receive what you need.

THE SYMBOLISM OF THE HEAD

The head has always been a symbol of authority, and in spiritual terms, it applies to both kingdoms, God's, and Satan's. An interesting example of this is when Jezebel, Ahab's wife, threatened to behead Elijah, the prophet, for having killed 450 prophets of Baal. (See 1 Kings 19). Later in the New Testament, the demonic spirit that operated in Jezebel reappears when the daughter of Herodias danced for Herod lasciviously, and because of the satanic enchantment at that moment, the king promised the young woman to give her everything she asked for, even if it was half of his kingdom.

"And when Herodias' daughter herself came in and danced, and pleased Herod and those who sat with him, the king said to the girl, "Ask me whatever you want, and I will give it to you." He also swore to her, "Whatever you ask me, I will give you, up

to half my kingdom." So, she went out and said to her mother, "What shall I ask?" And she said, "The head of John the Baptist!" ». **Mark 6: 22-24 (NKJV).**

A point worth highlighting, in the case of Elijah and John the Baptist, is that, although the attack came through two different women, the spirit that used them was the same: A spirit that reveals itself fiercely against whoever dares to challenge its malignity and seeks to leave without a head those who represent a threat to its interests.

When you release what you have, you receive what you lack.

On the other hand, we must consider that both Elijah and John the Baptist represented an authority in the spiritual world, revealing that this "spirit" has a special interest in those who are head and have authority in the spiritual world.

But this not only happened with these biblical cases. In the present day, we can see how this same "spirit" operates shrewdly through everyone who opens a door for it. It tries to entangle with its satanic charms, pastors, and leaders within the church and cause them to be affected and their families and the congregations that God has put them in charge of.

Everywhere there is a woman destined to destroy a man of God, and everywhere there is a man, being trained to ruin the ministry of some woman used of the Lord.

Because Satan knows and takes advantage of this truth very well: "If the shepherd is wounded, the sheep are scattered." (**Mark 14:27**).

So, this is the same strategic principle under which we must also operate in each of our battles, identifying the head or root of our conflicts and uprooting the evil from the very source where it comes from.

I began to exercise pastoral ministry at the age of seventeen. In all these years of ministerial work, I have realized that the enemy works in most conflicts that people face, not seeing the root of their struggles. This leads them to focus only on the superficial elements of the same, thus preventing them from identifying the current that is truly rocking the boat. Which, to better understand, I invite you to look at the following examples:

- ◆ Many consider that their debts are their problem when their origin is usually uncontrolled impulses, the desire to compete with others, or lack of guidance when making decisions that have to do with their finances. However, sometimes the root cause of indebtedness can even come from laziness towards work, negligence, or a high level of dependence on what is received from others. In these cases, instead of focusing only on the debts, the person must recognize the real cause of the situation and face it in the right way.

◆ Many believe the rebelliousness shown by their children is the problem. Still, sometimes the root of their rebellion may come from the people they relate to, be the product of a reaction to a particular crisis or arise from some pressure they have at home, such as the separation or divorce of their parents. Even the rebelliousness shown by some young people is sometimes a desperate cry for the attention they do not receive from their parents, which they tend to seek in the wrong way. In fact, the Hebrew word for "rebellion" is "meri" which also means bitterness or bitterness. And for these cases, the "stake" of prayer is the one that can pierce the head of this evil. The truth is, only prayer will break this oppression, and parents will receive the proper instruction to play their role in the right way.

DO NOT LOSE YOUR AUTHORITY BECAUSE OF SIN.

Sin takes place when the will to do good is changed by the intention to do evil.

Voluntary and premeditated sin is the worst kind of sin because it differs from sin committed under pressure.

The intentional repetition of sin without repentance is what causes a person's heart to harden and close his ear to the counsel given by the Lord through His Word and other people.

«*Speaking lies in hypocrisy, having their own conscience seared with a hot iron.* » **1 Timothy 4: 2 (NLT).**

The enemy cannot rob us of our spiritual authority, but we can surrender it to him through the continued practice of sin.

Sin takes place when the will to do good is changed by the intention to do evil.

Satan wants you to focus only on the carnal pleasure he offers you when his real plan through this is to bring death, destruction, and ruin into your life.

Finally, I want to refer to people who try to publicly maintain a "reputation" that cannot be sustained with their private life instead of renouncing and breaking with every sinful habit.

God's grace and anointing will not flow through those who refuse to forsake sin and who, not having the anointing of the spirit, proceed to make use of the "formulas" they already know to maintain the office, position, or reputation for which people recognize them, but this only works for them until God decides to unmask them.

On the other hand, the kingdom of darkness knows and only submits to people who walk in order and integrity. As an example of this, we have Paul. His anointing and authority were demonstrated to the point where people were healed, even when he touched the pieces of cloth people brought to him. So, when they were placed on the sick and demoniacs, they were instantly healed and delivered. (See Acts 19:11-12).

But while this was happening with Paul, a group of seven Jewish exorcists, all sons of a priest named Sceva, were so impressed with him that finding a man possessed by a demon, they applied to him what they had seen Paul do. But lacking the anointing and power he had, they decided to make use of the "formula."

So based on "formula," his words were as follows: "In the name of the Jesus whom Paul preaches, I command you to come out." The demon-possessed man looked at them and replied: «Jesus I know, and Paul I know about, but *who are you?* » *Then he pounced on the seven men, left them naked, and made them flee wounded.* **Acts 19: 13-16 (NIV).**

It is interesting to see how these itinerant exorcists thought that just by saying what Paul said, they could do what he did. But, on the contrary, they were put to shame. Instead of the unclean spirit coming out of that body (after having beaten and stripped those men), it was they who fled.

This story confirms that if what we say with our mouth is not attested by our actions, it is only mere words that are ineffective.

So do not play with sin or think that you can get away

with showing in public what you are not in private because sooner or later, you will be unmasked if you do not repent. This is what the proverb is referring to when it says:

«*Can a man take fire to his bosom, and his clothes not be burned? Can one walk on hot coals, and his feet not be seared?*» **Proverbs 6: 27-28 (NKJV).**

Chapter Principles

1. The fact that you feel you are just an ordinary person qualifies you to be used by the Lord in an extraordinary way.

2. We must authenticate the messages we preach by applying them to our own lives.

3. Everywhere there is a woman destined to destroy a man of God, and everywhere a man is being trained to ruin the ministry of some woman used of the Lord.

4. Many consider that their debts are their problem, when their origin is usually uncontrolled impulses, the desire to compete with others, or the lack of guidance when making decisions about their finances.

5. The rebelliousness shown by some young people is sometimes a desperate cry for the attention they do not receive from their parents, which they tend to seek in the wrong way.

6. Prayer breaks the oppression and brings parents the proper instruction to play their role in the right way.

7. Willful and deliberate sin is the worst type of sin because it differs from sin committed under pressure.

8. The intentional repetition of sin without repentance is what causes a person's heart to harden and close his ear to the counsel the Lord gives him through His Word and other people.

9. Satan wants you to focus only on the carnal pleasure he offers you when his real plan through that is to bring death, destruction, and ruin into your life.

10. God's grace and anointing will not flow through those who refuse to forsake sin, who, not having the anointing of the spirit, proceed to make use of the "formulas" they already know to maintain the position or reputation for which people recognize them.

11. If what we say with our mouth is not attested by our actions, it is only mere words without effectiveness.

12. Do not play with sin or think that you can get away with showing in public what you are not in private because sooner or later, you will be unmasked if you do not repent.

Ruth

You must let go of what is left behind to take what is ahead

R uth's name means "faithful companion or good friend," and apart from the woman described in Proverbs 31, she is the only one in the entire Bible who is called a "virtuous woman" (see Ruth 3:11). But this description had little to do with her origin, but rather with the good decisions throughout her life's journey. This also connected her to the glorious destiny God had reserved for her.

Her homeland was Moab, a pagan and idolatrous nation whose "god" was Chemosh, an idol to whom the Moabites worshipped, and in veneration of him, they sacrificed their children by throwing them into the fire. (**See 2 Kings 3:27**).

Based on this, we can deduce that both the mentality and the heart of the Moabites were totally contaminated, blinded, and distorted. A society capable of sacrificing its children in the fire to satisfy the demands of its idolatrous system does not have the slightest concept of value for the family. Here, much of the story of Ruth's life took place. In this land whose atmosphere was highly charged with hostility and perversity.

But what is the history of this nation? The origin of Moab arose when hundreds of years ago, Lot, Abraham's nephew, was given notice of the judgment that would come upon Sodom, to flee from that place with his family. However, as they were leaving, Lot's wife looked back and became a pillar of salt (see Genesis 19:26), while he and his two daughters continued their way, and once out of the land, they took refuge in the mountains. While there, Lot's daughters thought that their father and the two of them were the only people left in the land. So, to extend the offspring, they decided to get Lot drunk for two consecutive nights, and both slept with him, one the first night and the other the second.

After this act of incest, the two daughters became pregnant; the younger one bore a son whom she named Amon or Ben-Ami, from whom the Ammonites arose, and the older one bore a son whom she named Moab, from whom the Moabites arose. Thus originated these two nations, which became bitter enemies of Israel. In fact, concerning the nation of Moab, the following pronouncement was made, *"Terror and traps and snares will be your lot, O Moab,"* *says the Lord."* **Jeremiah 48:43 (NLT)**

On the other hand, Elimelech, whose name means "God is King" and Naomi, whose name means "Sweetness," lived in their hometown which was Bethlehem, and because of a famine that had visited the town, they went with their two sons, Mahlon and Chilion to dwell in the fields of Moab.

Mahlon's name means "languid," which some writers have argued may have been premature. While the name Quelion means "sick." While in Moab, Elimelech died, and after his death, both of his sons married Moabite women; the elder's wife was Orpah, and the wife of the younger was Ruth.

After approximately ten years of marriage, the two brothers died, leaving Naomi, and Orpah and Ruth, her two daughters-in-law, as widows.

After the death of the three men of this family, Naomi, hearing that God had visited Bethlehem to give them bread, decided to return there. When she set out on the journey, both daughters-in-law went with her, but on the way, Naomi stopped to exhort them to return to Moab, to return to the place where their roots, families, customs, and friends were because there they would find a husband.

On hearing this, both daughters-in-law wept and refused to return, but Naomi insisted. So Orpah kissed her good-bye, but Ruth stayed with her. And when Naomi insisted that she, like her other daughter-in-law, should return to her place of origin, she emphatically replied:

Today, very few people recognize and value those whom God has assigned to train and instruct them.

«*But Ruth replied, "Do not urge me to leave you or to turn back from you. Where you go, I will go, and where you stay, I will stay. Your people will be my people and your God my God. Where you die, I will die, and there I will be buried. <u>May the Lord deal with me, be it ever so severely, if even death separates you and me</u>." When Naomi realized that Ruth was determined to go with her, she stopped urging her.*»
Ruth 1: 16-18 (NIV).

This sounds powerful! And it turns out to be even more worthy of admiration when we remember that Naomi had become a bitter person because of all through which she had lived. Something that she reveals when she makes her return to the land of Bethlehem. (See Ruth 1:20).

At this point, we should note that very few people today recognize and value (as Ruth did) those whom God has assigned to train and instruct them, especially if they are complicated and difficult people. We have another example of this with Elisha. Although Elijah was a man subject to passions, he considered and honored him as a person of high value to fulfill his destiny.

Therefore, let us take the life of Ruth and Elisha as an example, and let us not let anything separate us from the divine connections that God has arranged for us; let us ignore their faults and focus on all that we can learn from them. God will use even the bad character they may sometimes show us to form us.

"If your boss is angry at you, don't quit! A quiet spirit can overcome even great mistakes." **Ecclesiastes 10: 4 (NLT).**

Ruth did not spare the adverse effects of following a bitter woman like Naomi because she loved her, honored her, and was willing to let God use her as the bridge to the destination. She had decided to turn her back on the land of Moab to reach. Although her origin was there, this place represented only pain, sin, and death.

Like Ruth, many are the people who will have to turn their backs on what they lived behind to conquer what lies before them. Because of certain past events, they are bitter, oppressed, and stagnant today.

Are you one of them? Are there things you would have wished never to happen in your past? Did you go through a difficult situation and still have not let go of the pain it caused you?

If so, you need to understand that no matter how difficult what you went through was, it did not have the power to kill you because if it had, you would not be reading this. So, if it could not kill you, thank God, because as you may have heard: *"What doesn't kill you makes you stronger."*

However, when you read this, you may say, "How easy it is for you to talk like

Very few people today recognize and value those whom God has assigned to train and instruct them.

that! When you have no idea what I have been through". In this regard, I will tell you that Satan bet would destroy me because I have gone through situations. But today, I can firmly and confidently tell you it is possible to overcome it. **You do not have to stay down. Learn to let go and let go**. Because even if it is not easy, it will always be possible when you decide that these situations are just part of a "chapter" and not the end of your story.

One of the reasons why many find it difficult to let go of the past is their tendency to cling to what is familiar to them. Therefore, they reject what is in front of them, even if it is much better than what was left behind.

And you, are you ready to leave your past behind? Are you ready to set out to conquer the new things that God has for you?

Do not give your "yesterday" the power to determine your "tomorrow," nor let where you come from determine where you go because it is more important how you decide to end than how you start.

Many are the people who will have to turn their backs on what they lived behind to conquer what lies before them.

Therefore, decide to be one of those who are willing to take its pieces into the hands of the Lord, no matter how much the past has beaten them so that He can make a work of art out of them.

Ruth's decision to leave Moab was the most important decision of her entire life, and the decision to leave your past behind is the most important decision of your entire life.

At this point, we must emphasize that leaving the past behind does not always mean letting go of the negative aspects. On the contrary, for many, their struggle lies in taking their eyes off their past successes and victories to move on to new conquests.

In the same order, some clung to a time in their life in which everything seemed to be stable, and in which some people were part of that "stability" who are no longer there, so now they believe that if everything does not return to the way it was before, their life is meaningless.

Something that, of course, is not true but a great lie that Satan seeks to weave in the minds of people, to which we must keep in mind the following principles:

+ Everything you once had was given to you by the Lord, and even if everything at one time is gone, you are left with the one who gave it to you, and he has all power to make all things new.

+ At times, God will cause some people to go away from you for a time and then bring them to you in an improved version. While at other times, it will be you that God will take you to a new level before giving them to you again.

- When the estrangement from someone or the denial
  of something has been permanent, thank God for the
  time you had and remember that what you call loss,
  Heaven sometimes calls the creation of space.

*"And we know that <u>God causes everything to work togeth-
er for the good of those who love God </u>and are called according to his purpose for them."* **Romans 8:28 (NLT).**

What you call loss, Heaven sometimes calls the
creation of space.

So, despite your past, learn to let go of what is left behind
and let the hand of the Lord guide you to what lies ahead.

Because if you try to move forward while you have your
eyes backward, your steps will be unstable, you will not be
able to keep your balance, and you will fall at any moment.

One of my favorite passages is where Paul, speaking to
the Philippians, says the following: *«No, dear brothers and
sisters, I have not achieved it, but I focus on this one thing:
Forgetting the past and looking forward to what lies ahead. »*
Philippians 3:13 (NLT).

This really inspires me because the term "forgets" used
in this passage according to the Greek translation is: "to
cause to lose the mind." Which denotes an action that Paul
decides to take and succeeds.

The way we think deter-
mines what we are. Our actions arise from our thoughts;
from actions, habits are created, character is formed,

*What you call loss, Heaven
sometimes calls the
creation of space.*

and character determines our destiny. (See Proverbs 23:7).

On another note, do not think of taking revenge on people whom the adversary has used to harm you. For even
though they may appear to be your enemies, they are only
collaborators in God's plans for you. Therefore, your "enemies" are not the problem. On the contrary, your real
problem is sometimes those who only seek your well-being
from a human point of view. Let us look at this example:

«*From then on, Jesus began to declare to his disciples that it
was necessary for him to go to Jerusalem and suffer much from
the elders, the chief priests and the writers; and be killed and
rise again on the third day. Then Peter, taking him aside, began
to reproach him, saying: Lord, have mercy on you; in no way
does this happen to you.* » **Matthew 16: 21-22 (KJV 1960).**

At this point, it is important to remember that Peter
was counted among Jesus' friends, those who sought his
"well-being." But Jesus, identifying the source from which
those words came, rebuked Peter severely, instead of thank-
ing him for his desire to take care of him: "*Get away from
me, Satan! You represent a dangerous trap for me, because
you see things only from the human point of view and not
from the point of view of God.* » **Matthew 16:23 (NLT).**

On the other hand, let us remember that Judas was considered as the traitor and the enemy, but when he was about to carry out his betrayal, Jesus told him: "But Jesus said to him, *"Friend, do what you have come for..."* **Matthew 26:50 (NASB).**

It is interesting to observe how the Lord calls his "friend" Peter "Satan" at such a crucial moment of his trial and calls the "treacherous" Judas "friend."

Those who you sometimes call "enemies" are the best friends of your purpose.

Regarding this, I have said on other occasions that although some think that this may have been an irony on the part of the Lord, I disagree because Jesus was never ironic.

It is more important how you decide to end than how you start.

Far from it, this expression shows, even being on earth as a human, He saw things exactly the way His father God saw them.

That is why at the moment Judas betrayed Jesus, even though everyone saw him as a traitor, Jesus saw him as his friend. For without Judas, there is no betrayal; without betrayal, there is no arrest; without arrest, there is no scourging; without scourging, there is no cross; without the cross, there is no death; without death, there is no resurrection; and without the resurrection, there is no victory.

Here it is demonstrated that those you sometimes call "enemies" are the best friends of your purpose. So, in the midst of your trials, you do not need people who feel sorry for you but who can see things according to the plans and purposes God has for you. For God never allows his children to be afflicted or grieved for nothing. (See Lamentations 3:33).

QUIT THE VICTIM MENTALITY

People with a victim mentality are those who always blame others for their events, saying:

"I am not happy because the person next to me does not make me happy" or "I cannot move forward because where I am at does not allow me to do so." This does not really correspond to their reality because God will never put our destiny in the hands of anyone else but Him and then ourselves.

So, instead of ceding the power to control your life to others, make use of the self-control the Lord has given you.

"For God has not given us a spirit of fear, but of power and of love and of a sound mind." **2 Timothy 1: 7 (NKJV).**

One of the things that the Lord has allowed me to develop is the ability to ignore everything that has the potential to stagnate me. This is because I have made a covenant with God that I will bear fruit for Him no matter what arises until the last day of my life.

In fact, as I write this book, I find myself going through a situation that I have been waiting for more than six years to resolve, but even this long and challenging process, I have not given the power to paralyze me. Because even though from the beginning it has been very painful. It has involved betrayal, disloyalty, different types of deceit, diverse abuses in its greatest expression, and a very long time of loneliness. The enemy has not stopped taking advantage to offer me different ways to escape from it; every time I pray to God for this, the only thing he tells me is: "Wait because it will be my hand and not yours that will get you out of this." And although it has certainly not been easy, and I have all the legal rights to get out of this on my own, I have laid my rights at God's feet and have decided to let only His perfect will take place in my life.

Those you sometimes call "enemies" are the best friends of your purpose.

And if you, like me, are waiting to see God's hand move on something, here are some principles to put into practice during the waiting time.

FOUR THINGS TO DO WHILE YOU WAIT

1. Take stock of your life and give value to what you have left: Looking at the story of Ruth closely, we can see a principle worthy of being applied in our time of waiting; and that is that even though she had no husband, no one to take care of her, she did not focus on what she needed, but on who needed her; she did not stop to see who could do something for her, but she set her sights on someone for whom she could do something. In other words, Ruth took stock of her life and saw that there was something left around her, someone to whom she could give her love, appreciation, and appreciation. That someone was Naomi, and it was the care and appreciation she showed for her mother-in-law that served as the bridge that led Ruth to reach the glorious destiny God had reserved for her.

Today, many women have ceased to appreciate what they still have left because of what they lack. Such is the case of those whose husbands have abandoned and have allowed this to drain and consume them in such a way that now their children not only have the father absent, but technically the mother is also absent. Because of her pain, she does not spend time with them, and if she does, it is with a bitter and indifferent attitude. Something that turns out to be highly unfair for the children because any process of separation of the parents usually affects them severely, and they do not always have the due maturity to face these processes. Still, they always hope to receive support from the part that remains necessary to help them face it.

There is someone around you who needs you, and there is something in your environment that you can dedicate yourself to.

So, if you are one of these women, I encourage you to quit that attitude today and decide to seek the Lord with all your heart.

Because in God's presence, your wounds will be healed, and your strength will be renewed so that you can focus and give the best of yourself to what you still have left.

But if you do not have children yet, and you do not have a mother-in-law like Ruth had, identify carefully what is it that you still have left? Because, even if you have not noticed, there is someone around you who needs you, and there is something in your environment that you can devote yourself to.

And it was Ruth's understanding of this that made her fame as a virtuous woman grow throughout the village. That reached the ears of a rich and kindly man named Boaz, who later became her husband and procreated Obed, David's grandfather, from whom came the line of Jesus Christ.

Thus, it was that Ruth's good deeds (who at one point in her life seemed to have nothing left) made her become the most illustrious and outstanding person in all the land of Moab. It also made her one of the four women mentioned in the genealogy of Christ.

Therefore, take stock of your life during the waiting time and give your best to what you still have left because you will be recognized tomorrow for the efforts you make today.

2. Use the wait as a training time: The time of waiting does not have to be one in which your whole life is put on hold, but you can take advantage of it to do many things.

Among them: affirm some area of your life in which you have neglected or strengthened relationships with family or friends from which you have been disconnected. You can also undertake a project or develop a habit that contributes to your well-being by exercising, reading books, or learning a language or trade. Finally, the fact that you find yourself waiting to see the manifestation of the Lord in something should not cause you to become a fruitless and unproductive person.

You will be recognized in the future for the efforts you make today.

People close to me, especially my family and work team, know that I am intolerant to lack of productivity and wasted time.

That is why while I am doing any line at any service station, I am always reading a book, taking notes for any lecture, or training I must give. I use all the hours I spend on airplanes and airports for writing or planning the different projects I work with, and when I have wifi on the plane, I use it to counsel the church members I pastor and communicate with the leaders who work with me.

In this way, I always try to make the most of every hour I have in the day, no matter what I do or where I am. Even when I am in my prayer time, I always have a

> *There is someone around you who needs you, and there is something in your environment that you can devote yourself to.*

notebook and pencil by my side to take quick notes of everything the Lord is directing me to do as I pray.

The reason for this is that I know the value of time, and I know that many things in life, when lost, can be replaced, but time is not one of them. So, a day that we waste is a day we can never get back.

But as I said before, this does not mean that I am not waiting to see the manifestation of the Lord's promise. It only means that I have made a firm decision to continually produce with my life the results that the Lord expects of me and not to let those results come to a standstill during the time that I am waiting on Him.

Likewise, I encourage you to make the most of your time and use the waiting to take your life to a higher level of development while your time is coming.

Because God is not preparing your blessings, He is preparing you so that you can handle them in the right way when you receive them.

Act as what God has already said you will be: <u>Unlike men, who first say and then do, God first does and then says.</u> **(See Isaiah 46:10).**

So, when you receive a promise from Him, you can have the full assurance that if you keep in obedience, surely what God has said He will do with you will be fulfilled.

Because of this, the third thing you can do while waiting is to start acting like what God has already said you are going to be.

We have an example of this in Joseph, who the Lord showed would be governor in a dream. But after this, every-

You will be recognized in the future for the efforts you make today.

thing that happened to him seemed to be contrary to what God had said he would do with him. Because of those dreams, his brothers said about him: Let us kill him! But God intervened by using Judah, his brother, so that instead of killing him, they sold him to the Ishmaelites as a slave, who in turn sold him to an officer of the Egyptian court named Potiphar.

It is almost certain that while Joseph was on his way to Potiphar's house, Satan whispered to him: "You will never become governor. You will have to be a slave for all your life. So, what good did it do you to dream if look where you ended up?"

But how did Joseph react to this? What did he do after receiving the vision that he would be governor? Did he find himself going through something different from that? Joseph kept within himself the image of what the Lord had shown him, and it was by keeping it alive internally that he was able to manifest it externally.

But how did he do it? By acting as the ruler Heaven had already said he would be, though he was only a mere slave by then.

So, because of God's backing with him and the high level of excellence he showed from the position he was in, not long after coming to Potiphar's house, he was appointed as the steward of all the affairs of that house.

Later, we see how Joseph was taken to prison because of the false accusation made by his master's wife. But even there, he did not act like a prisoner. Instead, he acted as the governor God had determined him to be. Dedicating himself to being a "problem solver," and because of this, he was able to notice when the faces of the cupbearer and the baker were sad due to the dreams they had.

Something worth highlighting is that because Joseph had the disposition to use the gift of dream interpretation while in prison, he is later sent for to do the same, but this time not to the king's servants but the king himself. So, the willingness to use the gift you have in your "prison" process will open the doors that will lead you to your destiny. As the proverbist expresses it by saying:

«*Giving a gift can open doors; it gives access to important people!*». **Proverbs 18:16 (NLT).**

After interpreting the dream to Pharaoh, Joseph was placed as the ruler of all the land of Egypt, fulfilling the promise that the Lord had given him years before.

4. Do not despair: The time of waiting is usually one of the most used opportunities by Satan to make us despair and throw us into his proposals, which, although sometimes do not seem to be bad, are certainly never the right ones. As we see in the case of Abraham and Sarah, whom God had told that He would give them a powerful offspring, but after waiting for ten years and not seeing the fulfillment of that promise, Sarah proposed to Abraham that he sleep with Hagar, her maid, doubting that what God had said could really come to pass. (See Genesis 16:3)

Error, which resulted in several consequences, among which are the ongoing conflicts that exist between Palestine, a nation made up of the descendants of Ishmael the son of Hagar; and between Israel, made up of the descendants of Isaac, the son born as a fulfillment of the promise God gave to Abraham and Sarah.

Therefore, no matter what promise you find yourself waiting for, renounce all anxiety and take no shortcuts. Because desperation can cause you to fall into things that are not part of

> *An empty chair will always be better than a chair occupied by the wrong person.*

God's plan for you, and once you find yourself in them, your desperation to get out is greater than it was before.

In the same order, do not be anxious to fill the empty spaces in your life in a hurry because an empty chair will always be better than a chair occupied by the wrong person.

God knows your need, and if you keep trusting in His faithfulness and care for you, the right person will come in due time.

« *"For I know the plans I have for you,"* declares the Lord, *"plans to prosper you and not to harm you, plans to give you hope and a future.* » **Jeremiah 29:11 (NIV).**

Chapter Principles

1. Let nothing separate us from the divine con-
    nections that God has arranged for us because
    God will use even the bad character, they may
    sometimes show us to form us.

2. One of the reasons why many find it difficult
    to let go of the past is their tendency to cling to
    what is familiar to them. Therefore, they reject
    what is in front of them, even if it is much bet-
    ter than what was left behind.

3. Decide to be one of those who, no matter how
    much the past has beaten them, are willing to
    take its pieces into the hands of the Lord so that
    He can make a work of art out of them.

4. At times, God will cause some people to walk
    away from you for a while and then bring them
    back to you in an improved version. While at
    other times, it will be you that God will take to
    a new level before giving them back to you.

5. If you try to move forward while keeping your
    eyes backward, your steps will be unstable, you
    will not be able to keep your balance, and you
    will fall at any moment.

6. Do not think of taking revenge on the people
    that the adversary has used to harm you. Be-

cause although they may seem to be your enemies, they are only collaborators of the plans that God has with you.

7. Without Judas, there is no betrayal; without betrayal, there is no arrest; without arrest, there is no scourging; without scourging, there is no cross; without the cross, there is no death; without death, there is no resurrection; and without the resurrection, there is no victory.

8. In your trials, you do not need people who pity you but who can see things according to the plans and purposes God has for you.

9. Many things in life, when lost, can be replaced, but time is not one of them. So, a day we waste is a day we can never get back.

10. God is not preparing your blessings. Instead, he is preparing you to handle them the right way when you receive them.

11. The willingness to use the gift you have in your "prison" process will open the doors that will lead you to your destiny.

12. Desperation can cause you to fall into things that are not part of God's plan for you, and once you find yourself in them, your desperation to get out is greater than it was before.

The Shunammite

A model worth imitating

U nlike the other women mentioned in this book, the Shunammite appears as a woman without a name. However, she is the only one the Bible defines as *"an important woman."*(See 2 Kings 4:8)

According to the Hebrew translation of the word "important," the word "khazac" used in this passage is translated as catch, be strong, courageous, help, fortify, obstinate, restrain, affirm, shelter, encourage, snatch, help, gird, confirm, grow, give, dedicate, detain, lay hold of, grasp, harden, strive, firm, strengthen, guide, invite, manage, maintain, show, resolute, retain, hold, have, take, overcome.

Many are the women who nowadays are busy following certain personalities of the cinema, art, or any other area of show business. Somehow, they are attracted to them, and they want to look or at least resemble one of them deep inside. To try to achieve this, they must follow them. They dress, comb their hair, put on make-up, undergo surgeries, and imitate their habits and behavioral systems to achieve it. Far from highlighting the value of women, they detract from it. Many of these actions are done only to exalt their self-image, attract the attention of the opposite gender, and compete with women of the same gender.

Now, at this point, I want to clarify that there is nothing wrong with dressing up and wanting to look good, but there is much danger in doing this just to highlight the ego or trying to imitate someone who lacks correct conduct. Because those who live their own way, and not the way God has established for them (even if it is hard for them to admit it), walk in darkness. And these people will never be able to guide those who seek to walk in the light. Thus, only when the precepts of Christ guide our life does it become a life worthy of imitation. Therefore, the apostle Paul, in all firmness, could say: *"Follow my example, as I follow the example of Christ."* **1 Corinthians 11:1 (NIV)**

But in the Bible, we find Paul as a model worthy of imitation and many other people who serve as examples and inspiration because of the way they lived. Such is the case of the illustrious Shunammite woman, whose name is not mentioned and whose physical attributes are curiously not mentioned either, but who is highlighted as a "model" truly worthy of imitation; here are just a few of them:

She knew how to take advantage of the opportunity

Most of the writings about this woman agree that she was wealthy and well-positioned. However, instead of thinking that she had everything because of her position, she did not pass up the opportunity to serve as a servant of the Lord, something that would later become the greatest of all her privileges. However, her intention to serve Elisha in the way she did was not motivated by the interest of receiving something in return from him since she had already received her blessing from God. But what did it mean that this woman sought to have this prophet in her house?

For better understanding, it is necessary to remember three highly prominent positions among the people in biblical antiquity: the king, the priest, and the prophet.

These people will never be able to guide those who seek to walk in the light

The king oversaw the direction and government of the people; the priest served as spokesperson of the people before God, while the prophet was the spokesperson of God before the people. For this reason, the prophet was considered the exact representation of God among the people.

Because of this, the Shunammite proposed to have the prophet Elisha in her house and consulted her husband to make room for him.

«*She said to her husband, "I know that this man who often comes our way is a holy man of God. Let us make a small room on the roof and put in it a bed and a table, a chair, and a lamp for him. Then he can stay there whenever he comes to us.*" » **2 Kings 4:9-10 (NIV).**

The Hebrew term for the word "let us make" used in this passage is "asa" and is defined as "building, constructing or manufacturing." This is even more interesting when we consider that in ancient times, the houses of wealthy people (as was the case of the Shunammite) always had several rooms and not just one room. That is, although it is certain that in the house of this woman there were one or more empty rooms (because she had no children to occupy them), she did not want to give to the one who was considered "the representation of God in the people," what she had leftover. Still, she wanted to take care and build him an inn, which even before being built, she saw it also furnished, and not only with a bed, but with other utensils that would be very useful for the office of the prophet, such as a table, a candlestick and a chair.

She consulted with her husband about what she wanted to do:

One of the qualities that most embellish a virtuous woman is recognizing her husband's rightful place, according to God's order. That is to say that no matter how wise, skillful, and intelligent she may be, if a woman is married, she must respect and honor her husband. As the apostle Paul expresses it when he says:

«*Wives, submit yourselves to your husbands, as is fitting in the Lord.* » **Colossians 3:18 (NIV).**

Now, at this point, it should be noted that the ideal design of subjection according to God's order is this:

"*For a husband is the head of his wife as Christ is the head of the church. He is the Savior of his body, the church.*" **Ephesians 5:23 (NLT).**

The only way that the lack of subjection to authority is not sanctioned is when it is aimed at harming and destroying those in its charge.

By comparing a wife's subjection toward her husband with the church's subjection toward Christ, we can understand that this command does not refer to an oppressive or abusive leadership on the husband's part. Instead, it brings covering, protection, and guidance to his wife. In the same way as being subject to Christ, the church finds protection, covering, and guidance in Him.

However, this does not mean that if your husband is not a Christian, you should not respect him and recognize him as the "head" of your home, because the fact that he does not fulfill God's command does not mean in any way that you should do the same. On the contrary, with your respect and submission to him, you will attract the attention of the Lord, who will bless you, seeing the disposition of your heart to obey, and will make your husband (even if he does not always recognize it) see in you, a true servant of God.

The only way that the lack of subjection to authority is not sanctioned is when it is aimed at harming and destroying those in his charge.

That was not the case for the Shunammite's husband. Because the text shows us how well this woman proceeded in recognizing her husband's authority and how he identified with her desires and shared with her in carrying out the good intentions that God had put in his heart.

«*She said to her husband,* "*I am sure this man who stops in from time to time is a holy man of God. Let us build a small room for him on the roof and furnish it with a bed, a table, a chair, and a lamp. Then he will have a place to stay whenever he comes by.* »** 2 Kings 4:9-10 (NLT).**

She was rewarded because of her care

The only way that the lack of subjection to authority is not sanctioned is when it is aimed at harming and destroying those in its charge.

As we mentioned earlier, the Shunammite woman's gesture toward the prophet Elisha had not been done to receive any special favor from him, something that is revealed in the following text:

«*Elisha said to Gehazi, "Tell her, 'We appreciate the kind concern you have shown us. <u>What can we do for you? Can we put in a good word for you to the king or the commander of the army?'" "No," she replied, "my family takes good care of me."*» **2 Kings 4:13 (NLT)**

But, although the intention of this woman was not to receive favors from the prophet, the Bible clearly states:

«*If you receive a prophet as one who speaks for God, you will be given the same reward as a prophet. And if you receive righteous people because of their righteousness, you will be given a reward like theirs.*». **Matthew 10:41 (NLT)**.

So after having refused to be recommended by Elisha to the authorities of his people, the prophet persists.

«*Later, Elisha asked Gehazi, "What can we do for her?" Gehazi replied, "She doesn't have a son, and her husband is an old man." "Call her back again," Elisha told him. When the woman returned, Elisha said to her as she stood in the doorway, "Next year at this time, you will be holding a son in your arms!" "No, my lord!" she cried. "O man of God, don't deceive me and get my hopes up like that." But sure enough, the woman soon became pregnant. And at that time the following year, she had a son, just as Elisha had said.* » **2 Kings 4:14-17 (NLT)**.

This confirms that taking care of God's things certainly results in God taking care of our things.

Now, at this point, it is important to emphasize that Elisha was a true prophet and not one who only had the name of a prophet. Something that we should consider, because today, many of those who call themselves "prophets" seek only the way to take advantage of any opportunity or relationship they have, thus making a terrible representation of the affairs of the kingdom of God.

While in the Shunammite's house, Elisha did not attempt to cross the boundaries that he knew he should have as a man of God.

In fact, he did not even approach this woman directly, but when he had to speak to her, he used his servant Gehazi as a means of approach.

Instead of being busy announcing who you are, let your deeds take care of revealing it.

On the other hand, Elisha's letter of introduction was the tremendous way in which God endorsed him. In fact, the Bible does not record that at any time, Elisha proclaimed himself a "prophet," and although the anointing he had was double that of his predecessor Elijah, he never boasted about it.

In the same way, instead of occupying yourself with announcing who you are, let your deeds oversee revealing it. For what good is it to say what you are when you do not have God's backing to support it?

Elisha said to the Shunammite: *"Next year at this time, you will be holding a son in your arms!" "No, my lord!" she cried. "O man of God, don't deceive me and get my hopes up like that." But sure enough, the woman soon became pregnant. And at that time the following year, she had a son, just as Elisha had said."* **(Verse 16-17).**

Elisha had no power in himself to make this miracle happen, but he needed to be backed by God for what he had said to become effective. And God manifested himself in favor of the Shunammite and her household, just as he had prophesied, according to the word spoken by his representative on earth.

«If the prophet speaks in the Lord's name, but his prediction does not happen or come true, you will know that the Lord did not give that message. That prophet has spoken without my authority and need not be feared.». **Deuteronomy 18:22 (NLT).**

Maintained a high level of control in the face of crisis and pressure:

Nothing tests our level of maturity more than the moments of crisis and pressure to which we are exposed. And it was the crisis that came to the Shunammite woman's house because of

Instead of occupying yourself with announcing who you are, let your deeds oversee revealing it.

her son's death that made it clear that the illustrious way this woman describes herself is not just a simple concept.

«One day when her child was older, he went out to help his father, who was working with the harvesters. Suddenly he cried out, "My head hurts! My head hurts!"

His father said to one of the servants, "Carry him home to his mother." So, the servant took him home, and his mother held him on her lap. But around noontime, he died. She carried him up and laid him on the bed of the man of God, then shut the door and left him there. She sent a message to her husband: "Send one of the servants and a donkey so that I can hurry to the man of God and come right back." "Why go today?" he asked. "It is neither a new moon festival nor a Sabbath." <u>But she said, "It will be all right."</u>» **2 Kings 4:18-23 (NLT).**

Before burying the child, she consulted the source from which it came:

The Shunammite's son represented the reward that God gave her through the prophet Elisha because of the attention she had shown for him; and the fact that she

> *Nothing tests our level of maturity more than the moments of crisis and pressure to which we are exposed.*

was aware of this was what made her go to the fountain from which the child came out, instead of burying him when her son died.

And you, what do you do when the blessing that God gave you dies m? What is your reaction when your children stray from the ways of the Lord? Or when the doctor tells you that you suffer from some incurable disease? Or when the bank sends you a notice saying that you are about to lose your house? What is the way you handle yourself when you discover that your partner has been unfaithful? Or when he decides to leave the house? Or when he asks you for a divorce without giving you many explanations?

These are just some of the faces that can come into our lives in times of crisis. But, although these times certainly hit us, shake us, and make it seem as if everything is collapsing, do not rush to give up; instead, follow the example given by the Shunammite, who, before burying her blessing, went back to the source from where that blessing came from.

Imagine how different this story would have been if this woman had proceeded to bury her son instead of going to the prophet. So many of the things that are dead in your life can be restored if you decide to present them before the Lord instead of accepting their current state as valid.

Connect with God amid your pain because only in Him will you find the answer you need to face whatever your situation may be. Because, although not in all cases the Lord's indication is the same (as we will see in the next chapter of this book), it is only by seeking God's answer amid your crisis that you will be able to receive the correct instructions about what to do, whatever your situation may be.

She did not want to disturb her husband with what was going on:

The way the Shunammite handled herself on this point is truly praiseworthy. As we said earlier, she was a submissive woman who showed her husband respect and consulted with him about the things she was going to do before doing them. But as a woman of revelation that she was, she avoided making comments to him that could affect his faith or incite him to give instructions that were not in accordance with the answer she could obtain by taking her case directly to where she would find God's answer.

"She sent a message to her husband: «"Send one of the servants and a donkey so that I can hurry to the man of God and come right back." "Why go today?" he asked. "It is neither a new moon festival nor a Sabbath." But she said, "It will be all right."» **2 Kings 4: 22-23 (NLT).**

She only discussed his issues with the right people:

Not all people have the maturity to give you the word or the directive you need to receive at certain times. Therefore, when it comes to talking about your problems, you must identify very well those whose level belongs to the "Gehazi" range; and those who, by their wisdom and degree of connection with the Lord, can give you a word according to God's will for you in those specific moments.

«As she approached the man of God at Mount Carmel,

Elisha saw her in the distance. He said to Gehazi, "Look, the woman from Shunem is coming. Run out to meet her and ask her, 'Is everything all right with you, your husband, and your child?'" "Yes," the woman told Gehazi, "everything is fine."

But when she came to the man of God at the mountain, she fell to the ground before him and caught hold of his feet. Gehazi began to push her away, but the man of God said, "Leave her alone. She is deeply troubled, but the Lord has not told me what it is. <u>Then she said, "Did I ask you for a son, my Lord? And didn't I say, 'Don't deceive me and get my hopes up?"</u>» **2 Kings 4:25-28 (NLT).**

Not all people have the maturity to give you the word or the guidance you need to receive at particular times.

Noticing how the Shunammite woman responds to Elisha's servant, some may think, "But she lied when she told Gehazi that everything was fine, when in fact her son was dead." But suppose we paraphrase what this woman said to Elisha's servant. In that case, we have the following: "Thank you for asking Gehazi, but the situation I have is beyond your ability to solve it."

Do not tell your affairs to everyone who asks you what is happening to you because many do not really care and only want you to inform them to please their curiosity. Even if they want to help you, others will not be able to do anything at all. In fact, it is even dangerous to tell your affairs to people who cannot guide you. Instead of helping you, the advice they give you may confuse you and cause you to make decisions that are contrary to what God expects you to make at that time.

However, this in no way means that you should repress yourself or that you cannot look for someone to unburden yourself to, but that you should open your heart only to the right people, as we see the Shunammite did. Then she said, «*"Did I ask you for a son, my Lord? And didn't I say, 'Don't deceive me and get my hopes up?"*» **2 Kings 4:28 (NLT).**

Going to those who have the right connection with the Lord in our moments of crisis and pressure will always cause us to be encouraged and well-directed, even if our solution is not always immediately forthcoming.

She was not willing to settle for anything other than God's perfect will:

So, while it is true that sometimes we do not find the way out of some moments of pressure in our lives, it is no less true that on other occasions, one of the things that can make a crisis even more complicated is to accept a solution that seems to be good and valid, but it is not the right one for our specific case.

Not all people have the maturity to give you the word or the guidance you need to receive at particular times.

In fact, even though it has been the way out for other people who have gone through a similar situation,

126

it does not mean that it is also the same in our case.

For example, the Bible tells us that with the cloths brought to Paul for him to touch, the sick were healed, and those bound with unclean spirits were set free. (See Acts 19:11-12).

But the Shunammite was not satisfied with the mere fact that Elisha gave Gehazi his staff to place over the child's face, even though the "staff" was considered a powerful instrument in the hands of a prophet. Because on it were recorded the references of miracles and events that took place during the career of that particular prophet.

So, by placing the staff on the face of the child, not only was an instrument that was always in the hands of Elisha but the promise that the Shunammite had been given was being placed on him, as well as the record of the fulfillment of the promise. But this did not resurrect him.

«Then Elisha said to Gehazi, "Get ready to travel; take my staff and go! Do not talk to anyone along the way. Go quickly and lay the staff on the child's face."

But the boy's mother said, "As surely as the Lord lives and you live, I won't go home unless you go with me." So, Elisha returned with her. Gehazi hurried on ahead and laid the staff on the child's face, but nothing happened. There was no sign of life. He returned to meet Elisha and told him, "The child is still dead."» **2 Reyes 4:29-31 (NKJV).**

But although she heard from the servant that the child did not revive, she still went to the prophet of God to give him the front of the dead son who was in hcr house.

And you, what do you do when, after certain attempts to save your situation, nothing happens? The Shunammite, accompanied by the prophet of God, continued her way home.

Likewise, when in adversity, all you hear are voices like these: "That disease has no cure, the debt you owe will never be able to pay it off, that son is already lost, or that man will never come back to you," do not stop your step. Ignore those voices and keep going.

Some battles must be fought with a stubborn attitude in order to be won.

«When Elisha arrived, the child was indeed dead, lying there on the prophet's bed. He went in alone and shut the door behind him and prayed to the Lord.» **2 Kings 4:32-33 (NKJV).**

This is one of the most relevant points in the whole story of the Shunammite woman. Because, in addition to her determination to see God's manifestation in her crisis, it shows that this was undoubtedly the miracle that demanded even more faith and perseverance from the prophet himself, since, at a particular moment, it seemed that nothing he did would bring any result.

Gehazi placed the staff on the child's face... *But the child did not wake up.*

There are things you will not see unless you firmly decide to stay in the fight until your miracle is manifested.

Then Elisha went into the room where the child was and shut the door and prayed to the LORD... *But the child did not wake up.*

Then he went up and stretched himself upon the child. He put his mouth upon his mouth, his eyes upon his eyes, and his hands upon his hands... *But the child did not wake up.*

After this, the prophet walked again and again through the house... But the child did not wake up.

However, instead of calling the Shunammite to give her his "heartfelt condolences" and help her accept her "apparent reality," Elisha **went back up** to the room where the child lay dead. He lay on him again, and after sneezing seven times, the child opened his eyes.

« *Then Elisha summoned Gehazi. "Call the child's mother!" he said. And when she came in, Elisha said, "Here, take your son!" She fell at his feet and bowed before him, overwhelmed with gratitude. Then she took her son in her arms and carried him downstairs.* » **2 Kings 4:36-37 (NLT)**

This is an extraordinary example that even if nothing in your situation seems to improve after doing everything you can and implementing everything you know (unless God determines you to do so), you cannot proceed to bury what has died to you.

In fact, it is noteworthy that the perseverance of the Shunammite not only resulted in the resurrection of her son. But even after several years, she was favored because of the same.

«Elisha had told the woman whose son he had brought back to life, "Take your family and move to some other place, for the Lord has called for a famine on Israel that will last for seven years." So, the woman did as the man of God instructed. She took her family and settled in the land of the Philistines for seven years. After the famine ended, she returned from the land of the Philistines, and she went to see the king about getting back her house and land. As she came in, the king was talking with Gehazi, the servant of the man of God. The king had just said, "Tell me some stories about the great things Elisha has done." And Gehazi was telling the king about the time Elisha had brought a boy back to life. At that very moment, the boy's mother walked in to make her appeal to the king about her house and land.

There are things you will not see unless you firmly decide to stay in the fight until your miracle is manifested

"Look, my lord the king!" Gehazi exclaimed. "Here is the woman now, and this is her son—the very one Elisha brought back to life!".

With the adversity you may be going through today, God is building a testimony that will bring blessing to your tomorrow.

"Is this true?" the king asked her. And she told him the story. So, he directed one of his officials to see that everything she had lost was restored to her, including the value of any crops that had been harvested during her absence."
2 Kings 8:1 (NLT)

This passage confirms that there is a supreme plan from the Lord behind everything that happens to us, whose purpose is to favor us. Although in the intense crises

In other words, with the adversity you may be going through today, God is building a testimony that will bring blessing to your tomorrow.

that hit us, it may not seem so in any way. In other words, with the adversity you may be going through today, God is building a testimony that will bring blessing to your tomorrow.

Finally, after considering all the wonderful lessons we have learned from this illustrious woman of Shunem, a worthy representative of the tribe of Issachar (see Joshua 19:17-18), we have no doubt that she has all the characteristics to be considered a true role model that all women today should seek to imitate.

"Then you will not become spiritually dull and indifferent. Instead, you will follow the example of those who are going to inherit God's promises because of their faith and endurance."
Hebrews 6:12 (NLT).

Chapter Principles

1. There is nothing wrong with dressing up and wanting to look good, but there is much danger in doing this, just to highlight the ego or imitate someone who lacks correct conduct.

2. Only when the precepts of Christ guide our life, it become a life worthy of imitation.

3. The result of taking care of God's things is that God takes care of our things.

4. Many of those who call themselves "prophets" seek only to take advantage of any opportunity or relationship they have, thus making a very bad representation of the affairs of the kingdom of God.

5. Elisha's letter of introduction was the tremendous way in which God backed him up.

6. Amid your moments of pressure and crisis, do not be in a hurry to give up; instead, follow the example set by the Shunammite, who, before burying her blessing, went back to the source from which that blessing came.

7. Many of the things that are apparently dead in

your life can be restored if you decide to present them before the Lord instead of accepting their current state as valid.

8. Not everyone has the maturity to give you the word or the direction you need to receive at certain times.

9. When talking about your problems, you must identify very well those whose level belongs to the "Gehazi" range and those who, because of their wisdom and degree of connection with the Lord, can give you a word according to God's will for you, at that given moment.

10. Going to those who have the right connection with the Lord in our moments of crisis will always encourage us and be well-directed, even if our solution is not always immediate.

11. When in adversity, all you hear are voices like these: "That disease has no cure, the debt you owe will never be able to pay it off, that son is already lost, or that man will never come back to you," do not stop your step. Ignore those voices and keep going.

Bathsheba

If God decided to take it from you... Let it go

All women, or at least most of them, have a secret to keep, something they have not divulged and have confided to absolutely no one. This is also true about their families because they all know something about their children, their husbands, or any other member of the family, that if it were to become known, it would affect the way many would see them. Unfortunately, things do not always go the way we plan in life. Sometimes our families and we make mistakes whose consequences we will have to learn to face because we have no way of turning back time to make amends. And, although these mistakes are forgiven from the very moment, we are ready to go to God and recognize our faults, Satan, in his continuous purpose of wanting to oppress us, uses them to accuse us, intimidate us, and shame us.

Something like this was what happened in the life of the woman we will deal with in this chapter, whose name is Bathsheba, which means "the seventh daughter or the daughter of the oath," who had as her husband a man named Uriah, whose meaning is "Jehovah is light."

Uriah, Bathsheba's husband, was an illustrious warrior in King David's army. The case involving this couple was considered the only blemish David had in his walk with the Lord.

«For David had done what was pleasing in the Lord's sight and had obeyed the Lord's commands throughout his life, except in the affair concerning Uriah the Hittite.» **1 Kings 15:5 (NLT).**

This establishes that the scriptures are faithful in declaring to us the faults, even of the people it applauds the most so that through their experiences, we can also be enlightened. But what was the situation in which these three characters were involved? To better understand, let us look at the following text:

"In the spring of the year, when kings usually go out to war, David sent Joab and the Israelite army to fight the Ammonites. They destroyed the Ammonite army and laid siege to the city of Rabbah. However, David stayed behind in Jerusalem.

Late one afternoon, after his midday rest, David got out of bed and was walking on the palace roof. As he looked out over the city, he noticed a woman of unusual beauty taking a bath. He sent someone to find out who she was, and he was told, "She is Bathsheba, the daughter of Eliam and the wife of Uriah the Hittite." Then David sent messengers to get her; and when she came to the palace, he slept with her. She had just completed the purification rites after having her menstrual period. Then she returned home. Later, when Bathsheba discovered that she was pregnant, she sent David a message, saying, "I'm pregnant." **1 Samuel 11: 1-5 (NLT).**

In the first place, it is interesting to consider that the circumstances that gave way to this sin were due to the negligence shown by King David towards his occupations as a ruler. He entrusted others with this task when he should have been with his troops on the battlefield. There is something that is exposed in the following expression "But David stayed in Jerusalem" (Verse 1). So, if he had been where he should have been and had taken care of what he had, David would not have been exposed to the temptation that dragged him to incur a sin that was increasing in terms of its level of iniquity. And all this later brought very unfortunate consequences to his life and his house.

Whenever we are out of the path of our duty, we are visited by a guest called "temptation," whose way of introducing itself is to make us set our eyes on things that, later, we end up regretting having looked at.

When David saw Bathsheba, he immediately gave free rein to his lust by sending for her. Although he was told that she was married to one of his most faithful soldiers, he did not stop his corrupt act, and once she was brought to him, he slept with her, and she became pregnant as a product of that act.

Because of the above, we can deduce that Uriah had already been absent from his home for some time because he was present on the battlefield where David was supposed to be. While being pregnant, Bathsheba knew that the act committed would not be hidden. Out of fear of the consequences, she told the king what her state was, knowing that she would be stoned according to the law if she had been taken to court. She did this, insinuating that it was his duty to do everything possible to protect her. So, David devised a plan to make Uriah look like the father of the child conceived and sent him out of the battlefield where he was to come and spend time with his wife.

When Uriah came to David, he used the pretext of having looked for him to find out the people's condition and the state of the war. After having talked to him enough to cover his true motives, he sent him home to rest with his wife, but instead of going home, Uriah preferred to sleep at the palace gate with the guards there. Something, of course, David was not counting on, so he sent for him for questioning because of this.

«When David heard that Uriah had not gone home, he summoned him and asked, "What's the matter? Why didn't you go home last night after being away for so long?" Uriah replied, "The Ark and the armies of Israel and Judah are living in tents, and Joab and my master's men are camping in *the open fields. How could I go home to wine, dine, and sleep with my wife? I swear that I would never do such a thing. »* **2 Samuel 11:10-11 (NLT)**

The next day at night, after failing in his first attempt to make Uriah sleep with his wife, he invited him to eat and drink until he became intoxicated. This already was an evil action because making a person drunk to deprive him of his reason is worse than stealing his money. But not even drunkenness made Uriah deviate from his purpose. He planned to stay away from his house and his wife until the army he belonged to finish the battle. This exposes the level of courage and commitment that this faithful soldier had, but not even having seen such a touching act of commitment and fidelity on the part of Uriah made David be moved. Still, on the contrary, when he saw his plan to make him look like the father of the child, he had conceived with his wife failed, Satan put it in David's heart to end the life of the innocent Uriah.

It is sad to see how the faithful soldier willing to die for his king was killed by his hand! Here it is clearly exposed how sin blinds the sight, hardens the heart, sears the conscience, and deprives those who commit it of all sense of honor and justice.

«So, the next morning, David wrote a letter to Joab and gave it to Uriah to deliver. The letter instructed Joab, "Station Uriah on the front lines where the battle is fiercest. Then pull back so that he will be killed".» **2 Samuel 11:14-15 (NLT)**

In this passage, we see how David's sin became viler with each procedure, to the point of making his victim a partaker in his death.

Shortly after Uriah died, David married his widow, and the child they had fathered was born. But God was not silent in this case because the fact that it was David did not make him fall into a preferential rank at the time of having to face the consequences that would come to him because of his sin. Although these consequences did not come until after a time, as part of God's mercy, to give David a chance to repent on his initiative, certainly the judgment of God came.

> *Sin blinds the sight, hardens the heart, sears the conscience, and deprives those who commit it of all sense of honor and justice*

And we know that a long time had passed after the sin had been consummated because when Nathan went to David, the child had already been born. In fact, the Bible does not tell us how old the child was when Nathan went to confront David.

As a confrontation, the prophet used as a story the case of a rich man who abused vilely a poor man, taking away the only sheep he had. When David heard it, he was reminded of a situation that happened with one of his servants or citizens of the town. So, he was ready to apply the full weight of justice to the guilty, which involved his death and restoring what had been stolen from the poor man four times. That is, multiplied by four. (See 12:1-6)

After hearing the king pronounce such "just" judgment on the guilty man, Nathan replied, "*You are that man. Thus, saith the LORD God of Israel, I anointed thee king over Israel, and delivered thee out of the hand of Saul, and gave thee thy Lord's house, and thy Lord's wives in thy bosom, and gave thee the house of Israel and Judah: and if this were not enough, I would have added unto thee much more.*

Wherefore then didst thou despise the word of the Lord and didst evil in his sight? Thou hast smitten Uriah the Hittite with the sword, and hast taken his wife to wife, and hast slain him with the sword of the children of Ammon. Therefore, now shall not the sword depart from thy house for ever, because thou hast despised me, and hast taken the wife of Uriah the Hittite to be thy wife. Thus, saith the LORD; Behold, I will bring evil upon thee out of thine own house, and will take thy wives before thine eyes, and give them to thy neighbor, and he shall lie with thy wives in the sight of the sun.

For thou didst it secretly: but I will do this thing before all Israel in the sunshine. And David said unto Nathan, I have sinned against the Lord. And Nathan said unto David, The Lord also hath forgiven thy sin: thou shalt not die.

But because thou hast blasphemed the enemies of the Lord in this thing, the son that is born unto thee shall surely die. And Nathan returned to his house... And on the seventh day the child died (**2 Samuel 12:7-15, 18**).

Note that this passage states that after seven days (not af-

141

ter the child was born, but after the message of the Lord was brought to David by the mouth of the prophet), the child died.

In other words, despite David's sincere repentance for his sin, prayer, and fasting that God, in His mercy, would let the child live (see 12:16), his death (unlike that of the Shunammite's son) had come as an irreversible determination on the part of the Lord.

Men may mourn someone's departure intensely, but they will not mourn for a long time.

But it is interesting to see David's attitude when he was notified of the child's death. For the Bible relates that he arose from the ground, and immediately bathed himself, perfumed himself, then dressed and went to the house of the Lord to worship. Then he returned to the palace, asked for food to be served, and ate, showing by this that he had found peace from God in the day of his affliction. (Ver. 12:20). But with Bathsheba, the same had not happened.

An important detail to note here is that men always tend to let go much more easily of things that are no longer there than women. In fact, we rarely hear a man whose wife has been gone for years say: "I am praying and fasting for her to come back.

Because after they have cried and suffered for a certain period, they proceed to fill the place left empty, no matter what their appearance is because even if they are tall or short, thin, or thick, attractive, or not so attractive, they will always find someone to fill that space.

Men may mourn someone's departure intensely, but they will not mourn for a long time.

I have been in pastoral ministry since I was 17 years old. To this day, I have never seen a man come to the front of a ministry and ask for prayer for his relationship to be restored, arguing that even though his former wife is now married and has children with another man, he still firmly believes that she is his wife. He still firmly believes that she will one day return to him and that all things will be restored because he knows that the man his wife now has is not the right one for her. After all, he is still the man she needs to have, and that even though she has left and married another man, he is still married to her in the same way; he remains married to her in the "spirit."

No dear sister! Men do not stay married to the "spirit" of a woman who has already made her life with another man. When it comes to them, if nothing happens in the "flesh," nothing happens in the "spirit" either.

But on the contrary, women can remain married for years in the "spirit," and although this is certainly not something that many understand, they cling to that feeling.

Now, at this point, I want to emphasize the following: Every woman to whom the Lord has given a promise of restoration for her marriage, no matter what she sees, must stand firm believing in that promise. Because if God said it, it will undoubtedly be fulfilled. Even if for man, it seems to be impossible. But it turns out to be something unfair and out of the Lord's plans for a woman to keep clinging to something He has already decided to take away from her. To stay emotionally attached to something He has already decided to take away and to spend years waiting for the return of something that God has determined will not return.

But how can a woman know if she should continue to wait or completely detach herself from something or someone that is no longer there?

To answer this, let us recall an important point from the previous chapter: To the Shunammite woman, whose son, after having died, the Lord raised him from the dead, the promise given to her about her son did not contain a pronouncement of death.

Therefore, if the Lord had not pronounced death in her particular case, she could not proceed to prepare a burial. Whereas in the case of Bathsheba's son, God, through the prophet Nathan, had clearly said: *"the son that is born to you shall surely die."* (Ver. 18)

So, as we said before, the answer as to whether you should continue to wait or completely detach from someone should be sought in prayer at the feet of the Lord. So, then, you can proceed under the guidelines of His perfect will for you in your specific situation.

I have seen many marriages restored by God, even when everything seemed to be lost, because a woman to whom God gave a word dared to wait and act according to that order. Still, I have also seen many women whom God decided to take someone away from them, waste valuable years of their lives waiting for the return of one who will no longer return by God's design.

Therefore, every woman who believes in the Lord must cling with all her strength to what God promised to resurrect (as the Shunammite woman did). Also, they must detach themselves with all dignity and firmness from what God has decided to cause to die (as it happened in the case of Bathsheba).

At this point, something very important to highlight is that such detachment does not have to be accompanied by hatred, resentment, or anger; but it must be done with the clear understanding that God is in control of what is happening and will take care of helping every woman who has to face it to overcome it. Because for every blow that life brings us, there is a special level of grace that comes from the Lord to help us overcome it.

After the child died, David got up from the ground, bathed, perfumed, dressed, and went to worship in the house of the Lord, but Bathsheba was still mourning. Some-

WOMAN REPOSITION YOURSELF

> *Because for every blow that life brings us, there is a special level of grace that comes form the Lord to help us overcome it.*

thing that was normal, of course, because she was the mother of the child. Also, because she must have felt the weight of guilt for what had happened, so this situation must have been excessively difficult for her to bear to such an extent that she even felt that her life had come to an end because of this.

But the same did not happen with David, because as we have already said, men have a different way of handling this type of problem. We can observe this even when they somehow hurt or affect a woman's emotions. Whether it is because of an act of adultery, or because his wife has discovered that she had a child out of wedlock, or because he has done something to her in some other way that has affected her. The response of a man after having asked for forgiveness (regardless of whether he has done it sincerely or not) is: "Forget about it. Don't bring it up anymore." For women, it is usually cruel because they tend to hold on to the pain, but for men, it is easy because that is the way they "usually" handle it.

And you, have you ever seen a man who has been involved with you in a crisis behave like he does not care about anything while you feel that everything is falling on you? If so, learn from them; tone it down and get over it. Now, here you may think for a moment. Oh yes, but how easy after all he did to me!

Cause I want to make it clear that in no way do I mean to imply that this is an easy thing to do, but I can firmly assure you that by continually punishing yourself with the same thing, you will make the matter much harder for you to bear.

David's ability to accept what God had determined is not only limited to the fact that he was able to bathe, eat, and dress himself after the child's passing, but most theologians agree that it was at that time that David wrote the psalm that reads:

"I rejoiced with them that said unto me. We will go to the house of the Lord." (**Psalms 122**)

So, David sang and rejoiced, but Bathsheba was still mourning.

And you, are you still mourning for something that you should have already overcome? Are you still attached to something that the Lord has already decided to detach from you?

Sometimes the person who left does not reject you because they want to, but because God has already decided to take them away from you.

If so, you must refocus, stand up, eat, bathe, and worship the Lord. Because you will not be able to move to the next level that God has prepared for you until you say goodbye to what He has already decided to take out of you.

So, do not beg for love or be willing to continue to be rejected by someone whom you should only proceed to bury. Because sometimes, the person who left does not reject you because they want to, but because God decided to take them away from you. So, if that person wants nothing to do with you, you should want nothing to do with them either. Say goodbye to that, move on, do not stay trapped in that situation, dust yourself off, and refocus. Dress up and get ready as best you can, show the best version of yourself, and do not insist on keeping alive what God has already decided that must die.

But how can we overcome the things that have caused us so much pain? The Bible says that after having been in the presence of the Lord, David went and comforted Bathsheba, a term that, according to the Hebrew language, is translated as encourage, calm, and make think. But what was King David's strategy to change Bathsheba's mind amid this terrible affliction? David led her to understand that despite the tragedy she had experienced, something new could come out of it.

Sometimes our greatest victories come from our greatest mistakes.

So, after repenting, we see how not only God allowed them to conceive again, but from the very womb of shame, he arranged to give birth to King Solomon, the wisest of all the kings of the Earth and through whom the offspring was sustained that brought forth the birth of our Lord Jesus Christ. (See Matthew 1:6).

This is very relevant because we cannot say that God used Uriah's wife to bring Solomon because He did not find anyone else to use for this purpose. For He could have used Abigail, Michal, or any of the hundreds of concubines David had, for that purpose. But even with all these options, he decided to use the woman of error, who at one time had gone through a severe crisis that had brought death to something she loved, to proceed later to give life to what she still carried in her womb.

How wonderful it is to see how God can bring glory even from our mistakes when we recognize our sins and humble ourselves before Him!

For He is immediately ready to forgive our failures and make those mistakes, far from destroying us, serve to make us stronger, wiser, and firmer than we were before we made them. In fact,

Because you will not be able to move to the next level that God has prepared for you until you say goodbye to what He has already decided to take out of you.

sometimes, our greatest victories come from our greatest mistakes. So instead of believing that all is lost when you make a mistake, humble yourself before the Lord, dust yourself off, and move forward. God is an expert at taking our mistakes and transforming them into testimonies.

On the other hand, we cannot fail to mention the fact that possibly because of her past, Bathsheba may have been singled out by David's other wives, by one of his concubines, or by anyone else around her, who may not have made much effort to hide their singling out. But the fact that the Lord chose her to be one of four women mentioned in the genealogy of Christ shows us that Bathsheba became resistant to the murmurings, accusations, and all the other confrontations that could have been made against her because of her error. So, if you, like her:

You are being challenged because of some loss... Become resilient!

If you are part of a scandal... Become resilient!

If you are being rejected because of some mistake... Become resilient!

Even if they underestimate you and only talk bad about you... Become resilient!

Even if they throw hints at you and roll their eyes in front of your very face... Become resilient!

Ignore everything that has the intention of hurting you and focus on giving birth to the king you carry in your belly. Because, although many expect this situation to mark the end of your existence, they ignore this was only part of a chapter of your life; and that the same

Sometimes our greatest victories come from our greatest mistakes.

woman of error in one chapter can become the woman of honor in the next.

So, even though you may have gone through a divorce, even though you may have been removed from the position or office you held; and even though your reputation may have taken a hit because of failure, this is just part of a bad chapter. But your story does not end here.

"For behold, I do a new thing; it shall soon come to light..." **Isaiah 43:19 (NKJV 1960).**

Satan will always look for ways to make you think that your adverse situation represents the end of you, but do not believe him because if Bathsheba's end had come because of her crisis, she would have died along with the child. On the contrary, she stayed alive because God had planned to do something greater with her than the mistake she had made.

So if you are a survivor, and even after all the terrible things that have happened to you, you are still standing, it is because the Lord has not yet finished His plan with you despite the mistake you made and over and above whatever loss you have had; and if He has not yet finished it, neither can you.

So, this very day dry your tears, regain your strength, and let the process, instead of ruining you, be used by

The same woman of error in one chapter can become the woman of honor in the next.

the Lord to bring out the "king" in you.

"For this is the time God has chosen to give us salvation, to comfort the sorrowful, to change their defeat into victory, and their sorrow into a song of praise. Then they will call them: Victorious oaks, planted by God to manifest His power." **Isaiah 61:2-3 (NLT).**

Chapter Principles

1. Sometimes our families and we make mistakes and commit errors whose consequences we will have to learn to face because we have no way of turning back the clock to make amends.

2. The scriptures are faithful in declaring to us the faults, even of the people whom it applauds the most so that through their experiences, we too can be enlightened.

3. Whenever we are off the path of our duty, we are visited by a guest called "temptation," whose way of introducing itself is to make us set our eyes on things that, later, we end up regretting having looked at.

4. Men do not remain married in the "spirit" to a woman who has already made her life with another man. Because when it comes to them, if nothing happens in the "flesh," nothing happens in the "spirit" either.

5. It is unjust and out of the Lord's plans for a woman to hold on to something He has already decided to take away from her. So, likewise, to remain emotionally attached to something He has already decided to take away and spend

years waiting for the return of something that God has determined will not return.

6. The answer as to whether you should continue to wait or completely detach from someone who is no longer with you must be sought in prayer at the feet of the Lord so that you may proceed under the guidelines of His perfect will for you in your specific situation.

7. The duty of every woman who believes God is to cling with all her strength to what He promised to resurrect (as the Shunammite did) but to detach herself with all dignity and firmness from what He has decided to cause to die (as happened in the case of Bathsheba).

8. Do not beg for love or be willing to continue to be rejected by someone whom you must only proceed to bury. Because sometimes, the person who left does not reject you because they want to, but because God has already decided to take them away from you.

A Woman's Ministry

Forbidden by God or rejected by men?

One of the most debated biblical topics in recent times is the role of women in the ministry, which has now re-emerged with much more strength despite having been dealt with in other times. Bringing several confrontations between those who are for, and those who are against, the ministerial exercise of women, but also leaving great confusion in many women who wonder: Is it true that I cannot exercise my ministry? And if not, to what extent can I work in the work of the Lord?

So, with the intention of shedding light on this apparent "dilemma," we will proceed to explore its main implications. But not to contradict or misrepresent in any way what has already been established by God. On the contrary, with the healthy intention of seeing the authentic instruction that the Bible gives us regarding this, in the light of His Word.

What God said about man in the beginning also had a direct reference to women.

So, to establish the proper foundation, before going straight to the subject, it is important to remember that when God created "man" in the beginning, the woman was already within man from the very moment he was created, even though she had not yet been revealed. Therefore, what God said about man in the beginning also had a direct reference to women.

"Then God said, "Let us make mankind in our image, in our likeness, so that they may rule over the fish in the sea and the birds in the sky, over the livestock and all the wild animals, and over all the creatures that move along the ground." So, God created mankind in his own image, in the image of God he created them; male and female he created them." **Genesis 1:26-27 (NIV).**

But let us observe what we are also said further on... *"In the day that God created man, He made him in the likeness of God. He created them male and female and blessed them and called them Mankind in the day they were created."* **Genesis 5:1-2 (NKJV).**

So, although the manifestation of the woman took place in Genesis 2:22 where it tells us: *God did not have to take dust off the ground again to reveal the woman. Instead, he took a part of the man he had already created.*

«Then the Lord God made a woman from the rib, and he brought her to the man. »

His creation took place together with the creation of man in Genesis 1:27, where it is revealed to us:

"And God created <u>man</u> in his own image; he created him in the image of God. <u>Male and female he created them</u>." **(NIV)**

In these passages, it is clearly established that the creation of man, in the beginning, refers to the whole human race, although by then, it was only contained within a single body, which was that of Adam.

Therefore, the expression "let us make man to rule" does not refer only to Adam but also Eve, who was already contained within him.

Therefore, God did not have to take dust off the ground again to reveal the woman. Instead, he took a part of the man he had already created. In fact, the Hebrew translation used for the term "let us make," used in Genesis 1:26, alluding to the creation of man, is "asa" and is translated as "build." While the Hebrew word used in Genesis 1:22 referring to the making of the woman is "bana" and is translated as "rebuild."

But what is the implication of this? To build is: To found or establish an entity. While to rebuild is: To remake based on what was made.

So, God did not qualify her as an inferior being to man but positioned her as his companion and complement.

But this being biblically proven, then, where do the passages found in two of Paul's letters about women's ministry come from?

To present the proper answer to this question, let us proceed to consider the content implied in these texts.

Considering the texts (Part One)

"Women should be silent during church meetings. It is not appropriate for them to speak. They should be submissive, as the law says. If they have questions, let them ask their husband at home, for it is not proper for women to speak in church meetings." **1 Corinthians 14:34 (NLT).**

Paul's letters to the Corinthian church contain some of the most well-known and cherished passages for Christians of all times, such as the Hymn to Love, the institution of the Lord's Supper, and the exposition of the Resurrection. But some of us cannot deny that sometimes we have difficulty following the thread of these letters. It seems to us that they intermingle the themes and make us perceive the deep feeling of Paul's heart (both for the glory and for the problems of that church), which was probably the one

---

Therefore, what God said about man in the beginning also had a direct reference to women.

158

that gave the apostle the most headaches; something that we cannot fail to consider if we truly want to have the correct interpretation of the mentioned text.

For example, in his first letter to the Corinthians, Paul mentions several matters this church had written to him. And before answering their questions, the apostle first refers to what they had previously written or asked him and then proceeds to present his response. This pattern of first mentioning what they had written to him and then issuing an answer begins in chapter seven and continues through chapter fourteen of this letter.

Letting the readers know that he would deal one by one with all the matters about which they wrote to him, and the first to be pointed out was the church's own appreciation of conjugal relations, to the point of considering it possible to establish abstinence from the act as a norm.

So, to answer this position of the church, Paul first repeats their statement verbatim, just as they had written it to him.

God did not have to take dust off the ground again to reveal the woman.

"Now regarding the questions you asked in your letter. Yes, it is good to abstain from sexual relations. But because there is so much sexual immorality, each man should have his own wife, and each woman should have her own husband." **1 Corinthians 7:1-2 (NLT).**

As we can clearly see in this passage, when Paul said: "that it would be better for man and woman not to have sexual relations," he was only referring to what they had told him before. Although he recognized that abstinence (if possible) would be good for consecration purposes, that level of consecration corresponds to a special calling from God and does not apply to all men. (See Matthew 19:12).

So, Paul's response to this statement of the Corinthians was: *"In reference to what they wrote to me, I will tell them, that because of fornications, let each man have his own wife, and let each have her own husband."*

If we overlook the dialogue in this letter, which is maintained throughout its development, we can conclude that Paul required Christians to live a life of celibacy. If so, what the Corinthians proposed would have been accepted by the apostle, without any caveats, and would have been used to be preached as a rule of life in all church pulpits.

But it is God's design that man should marry because marriage was instituted by Himself.

While knowledge makes us feel important, it is love that strengthens the church.

So, in short, Paul said: "(Although we recognize that there are those with a special call to separation) because of fornications, let each man have his own wife, and let each woman have her own husband."

Once he gave this answer, the apostle turned to other areas in which the church also needed direction, and the next matter about which the church had written to him is found in chapter eight.

> *But it is God's design that man should marry because marriage was instituted by Himself.*

"Now <u>regarding your question about food that has been offered to idols.</u> Yes, we know that "we all have knowledge" about this issue. But while knowledge makes us feel important, it is love that strengthens the church." **1 Corinthians 8:1 (NLT).**

The matter of meals offered to idols was a subject in question for the Corinthians considering their Christian liberty, to which for Paul to refer, he again repeated the point they had earlier made to him.

Later, in chapter 10, the apostle maintains the same line of clarification by saying, "For I would not have you ignorant, brethren, that our fathers were all under the cloud, and all passed through the sea..." Again, warning the church about idolatry.

While in chapter 11, he instructs them about the way women should dress and the way the Lord's Supper should be taken; in chapter 12, he speaks about the use of spiritual gifts, and to give continuity to the letter, he makes a masterful exposition about love in chapter 13.

In chapter 14, he adds additional instructions about the spiritual gifts, focusing especially on the gift of Prophecy. At this point, it is interesting to consider that when the apostle instructed the church about the gifts of the Spirit, he said that "all," both men and women, can prophesy so that "all" men and women can learn and be comforted.

"In this way, all who prophesy will have a turn to speak, one after the other, so that everyone will learn and be encouraged." **1 Corinthians 14:31 (NLT).**

So, the instruction given here by the apostle Paul directly contradicts what is recorded in verses 34-35 when he says:

"Let your women keep silence in the congregations, for it is not permitted to them to speak, but let them be subject, as also the law says. And if they want to learn anything, let them ask their husbands at home; for it is unseemly for a woman to speak in the congregation".

This statement was not an affirmation on Paul's part, but as we have already seen, he only mentioned it as something they had told him before and then gave his answer. Which, of course, had to be coherent with what in the same chapter, he had exposed, saying:

Everyone can prophesy!

Everyone can learn in the church!

Everyone can be comforted in the church!

Paul was an extremely educated man. He spoke Hebrew and Greek fluently and was intelligent enough to distinguish the word "all" from the word "some" or to simply issue a statement saying: "You men can prophesy."

According to Strong's Concordance, the Greek word "all" refers to any allusion of the "all." This includes all forms of inclination and all forms of means because, according to this grammatical root, "all" refers to the absolute of something. In this case, the term alludes to the "all" of the church, composed of men and women.

In other words, if Paul had wanted to limit the public gift of prophecy to men only, he would have done so. Instead, however, after mentioning what they had told him, as he had done in the previous chapters, he proceeds to give his answer.

And, of course, when a person is writing in continuous mode, he does not have to elaborate a prologue based on what was previously said. So since Paul had made it clear that in every point to be made, he was referring to what they had mentioned to him before, in addressing the subject in verse 34, what Paul basically says, is the following: "Now this is what you said to me: Let your women keep silence in the congregations; for it is not permitted to them to speak, but let them be subject, as also the law says. And if you want to learn anything, ask your husbands at home; for it is a dishonest thing for a woman to speak in the congregation" (position of the Corinthians), to which Paul replies:

"What, has the word of God gone out from you, or has it come to you alone? If any man thinketh himself to be a prophet, or spiritual, let him acknowledge the things which I write unto you: for they are the commandments of the Lord. But he who is ignorant, let him be ignorant. Therefore, brethren, give diligence to prophesy, and forbid not to speak with tongues". **1 Corinthians 14:34-39.**

At this point, we must emphasize that it is not possible that the apostle Paul in verse 31, told the Corinthians that everyone could prophesy, and then, in verses 34 and 35, orders that women keep silent in the church because it would be an illogical contradiction within the same text.

So again, the apostle Paul referred to what was quoted by the Corinthians.

Something that, in the case of some writers who write differently, one could argue that they seem to contradict themselves because they forgot what was previously stated or because they changed their way of thinking because of circumstances or social pressure. But here, Paul is writing all his answers in one letter, addressed to the same church, within the same context.

And as for the Corinthians' absurd assertion about the ministry of women in the church, Paul responded with two pertinent questions:

1. *Did the Word of God come from you?*

2. *Did it (the Word) come to you only?*

Instead of approving of their position concerning women's ministry in the church, he questioned them with the following: What are you saying? Did the holy and unbiased Word of God come from you? Are you saying that you are the cause and source of the Word of God?

But in addition to rebuking the pride and arrogance of these misinformed men, Paul told him that if they considered themselves to be prophets and spiritual, then they should accept what he had written as the command of the Lord, their Master, and not of him as a man.

If these questions are not accepted as an answer to the above prohibition presented by the Corinthians, then Paul would be making an inference in the text, which does not fit the argument. Actually, let us observe the way this version expresses it: *"Did the word of God come from you? Did it come to you only?"*

Another important element, which serves as further evidence that Paul was only repeating their statement, is that neither in the Old nor the New Testament is there any law commanding women to keep silent in the church.

So, the "law" mentioned here was not the Torah law, established by God for the people, which is composed of the first five books of the Old Testament, written by Moses.

To be well grounded, it is fundamental to maintain a balance between the movement of the Spirit and the handling of the Word.

Because if so, we would have biblical evidence about this.

The Corinthian church had been provided with the gifts of the Spirit. Still, despite this, they were spiritual "babies" in terms of understanding, so it was a church with terrible problems of confusion between pagan customs, human doctrines, and the Law of God.

This shows that, although the gifts are present in a church, there is the need to have mature leadership among those who have reached real growth and understanding in the Word of God because it is fundamental to maintain a balance between the movement of the Spirit and the handling of the Word to be well-grounded.

Considering the texts (Part Two)

"And I do not permit a woman to teach or to have authority over a man, but to be in silence." 1 Timothy 2:12 (NKJV).

Before proceeding to explain this passage, to establish the proper foundation, we must remember what we saw at the beginning of this chapter about the creation of man: that God, at the moment of creating man, "created them male and female" and united them into one flesh. (See Genesis 1:27) And although Adam was the first to be revealed (for which reason, according to God's order, it is incumbent upon him to go before in hierarchical order), both were given dominion over all living creatures. In the same way that judgment fell upon both after sinning.

Being part of the punishment for the woman's sin, that the man would rule over her "... *And thy desire shall be to thy husband, and he shall rule over thee*". (**Genesis 3:16).**

A statement that is and will continue to be part of the order that God has established for the home, but that has been reformed based on the direction of Jesus Christ:

For "For the husband is head of the wife, as also Christ is head of the church; and He is the Savior of the body." Ephesians 5:23 (NKJV).

At this point, we cannot overlook the fact that male sovereignty was established as part of the husband-and-wife relationship in the home and not in the church. For no man has ever been made head of the church, but this position belongs to Christ alone.

"But I want you to know that the head of every man is Christ, the head of woman is man, and the head of Christ is God." **1 Corinthians 11:3 (NKJV).**

In this portion of Scripture, the apostle Paul's instruction again refers to God's order for the home and not to the ordering of ministries within the church.

No man has ever been head of the church, but this position belongs to Christ alone.

Making it clear once again that the head of the woman is the man, but the head of every man must be Christ.

Therefore, the husband has an immense responsibility, which is to surrender his own head (mind, will, government) and let himself be guided by the Sovereignty of Jesus Christ because he should not have the government of two powers: "that of his own carnal mind and that of the Spiritual Sovereignty," but he has to choose between his own head or that of Christ, and it is by letting himself be guided by Jesus Christ, that he becomes the suitable head to bring instruction to his wife and his home.

Thus, according to God's order for the home, the woman has no "head" of her own but must be united to the man, who is her head. But this does not refer to the rule of a carnal head. Instead, it refers to the headship of a man who, in turn, is guided by Christ, whose head is God.

It is fundamental to maintain a balance between the movement of the Spirit and the handling of the Word to be well-grounded.

There will never be true unity and peace in the home as long as two heads, two minds, and two wills try to rule and direct.

So, just as the wife must be subject to her head which

is her husband, he, in turn, must be subject to his head, who is Christ. In this way, the Sovereignty of Christ will be in control, and this type of Christian home will be dominated by the unity, harmony, and peace of God.

Having said this, let us now take a closer look at what the Apostle Paul said when speaking to his disciple Timothy. And to be more precise, we will make use of the meaning in the Greek language in the relevant terms of this passage.

As long as the Lord directs it, the husband's direction will produce a calm attitude in his wife to receive from him all that he imparts to her.

According to the Greek translation in this passage, the woman is "gune," which translates as "married or wife" let her learn in silence, with all subjection. For I do not permit the woman ("gune": married or wife) to teach, nor to take authority over the man who according to the Greek translation in this passage is "aner" and is translated as "husband or husband." (1 Timothy 2:11-12).

For no man has ever been made head of the church, but this position belongs to Christ alone

As we can notice, the translation of the terms "man and wife" according to the Greek confirms that this indication refers exclusively to God's design for the home and not to the woman's ministry in the church.

God has placed the responsibility of leadership in the home on the male "husband." But as we have already said, he must first allow himself to be guided by the direction of Christ to fulfill the function of head of his wife, as established by the Lord. And as long as the Lord directs it, the husband's direction will produce a calm attitude in his wife to receive from him all that he imparts to her.

Having said this, let us proceed to the next point referred to in this passage.

"For it is not permitted for the woman (wife) to teach or take authority over the man (husband) but to be quiet." (Verse 12).

The term "silence" according to the original language is "jesujia" and is translated as "quietly."

The word quietly means free from rebellious thoughts and feelings. So, it should never be disputed that the wife should learn in a gentle spirit and subject to her husband, who is her head.

There will never be true unity and peace in the home as long as two heads, two minds, and two wills try to rule and direct.

However, there is only one man whom God has set over the woman, and to whom she is to submit, and that is her husband; from whom she is not to usurp authority but is to submit to him in the home and learn from him with gentleness what is revealed to him because of having Christ as the head.

And wives must pray every day that their husbands assume this position in their relationship with Christ. For it is not easy for many of them to surrender their will and their own ideas to submit to the Lord's guidance.

Couples grounded in Christian values should set aside their own carnal sovereignties and properly implement the order established by God for the home through the headship of Christ, which should be manifested through the headship of the male, for there would be no conflict if the order of every home proceeded directly from the Lord's direction.

As we mentioned before, the carnal and natural lordship of man was part of the curse of sin for the woman, but that changed after the sacrifice of Jesus Christ. For

The husband's direction will produce a calm attitude in his wife to receive from him all that he imparts to her.

on the cross of Calvary, He redeemed us from the curse of the law, and paid for our sins by being made a curse for us. (See Galatians 3:13)

So, the children of God are no longer under the curse. Instead, they have been redeemed and delivered through the Lord's sacrifice.

On the other hand, we should note that the verses that follow confirm that the instruction given by Paul to Timothy applies exclusively to the relationship of man and woman in the home.

"But she will be saved by begetting children, if she continues in faith and love and sanctification with modesty" **(1 Timothy 2:15).**

If we insist on confining this statement within the text of the church, then we would say that the woman's salvation would depend on her ability to bear children, which turns out to be an unacceptable explanation according to the whole revelation of the Holy Scriptures.

But then, why did the apostle Paul say this? Here, the apostle undoubtedly referred to Eve's transgression, recalling the punishment she received after having sinned. To the woman, he said, *"I will greatly multiply the sorrows of thy conception; in sorrow, thou shalt bring forth children."* **(See Genesis 3:16)**

There is only one man whom God has set over the woman, and to whom she is to submit, and that is her husband.

Therefore, when we study the Word of the Lord and understand it within its context, we do not find any contradiction in the teachings it contains. Therefore, as we have been able to appreciate through these biblical passages, women can minister the Word in the church, but according to the order established by God, married women should let themselves be guided by their husbands and learn from them in the home, as long as they are guided by the one who should be their head, which is Jesus Christ.

Having said this, it is of order to clarify that for the consideration that we have made of this subject, we consider two important rules of Hermeneutics, which are the following:

1. **The Bible is its own interpreter.**

2. **To consider a biblical point as doctrine, it must be supported by at least three biblical verses.**

Therefore, in the case of considering the impediment of the ministerial exercise of women as a doctrine, since there are only two verses that allude to the subject (according to the Hermeneutics), it does not have the

The children of God are no longer under the curse. Instead, they have been redeemed and delivered through the Lord's sacrifice.

requirements to be observed as such. Furthermore, let us remember that the word of God does not contradict itself. So, if God really did not approve of the ministry of women, we would not have so many cases in the Bible that demonstrate the contrary. Let us look at just a few of these...

Old Testament examples:

♦ **Miriam, the sister of Aaron and Moses:** *"And Miriam <u>the prophetess</u>, Aaron's sister, took a tambourine in her hand, and all the women went out after her with tambourines and dances."* **Éxodus 15:20 (NKJV 1960).**

♦ **Deborah the judge and prophetess:** *"Now Deborah, a prophetess, the wife of Lapidoth, was judging Israel at that time.".* **Judges 4:4 (NKJV 1960).**

♦ **Hulda the prophetess:** *"Then went Hilkiah the high priest, and Ahikam, Achbor, Shaphan, and Asaiah, unto <u>Huldah the prophetess</u>, the wife of Shallum... And she said unto them, <u>thus saith the LORD God of Israel</u>, Tell ye the man that sent you unto me..."* **2 Kings 22:14-15 (NKJV 1960).**

The example of Huldah is fascinating because Josiah being a godly king, Hilkiah being a high priest, and Jeremiah being a prophet contemporary with her, the answer that both the king and the people needed came specifically through this woman.

New Testament examples:

♦ **Philip's four daughters:** *"On the next day we who were Paul's companions departed and came to Caesarea, and entered the house of Philip the evangelist, who was one of the seven, and stayed with him. <u>Now</u>*

this man had four virgin daughters who prophesied."
Acts 21:8-9 (NKJV).

♦ **Junia the Apostle:** *"Greet Andronicus <u>and Junia,</u> my fellow Jews, who were in prison with me. <u>They are highly respected among the apostles</u> and became followers of Christ before I did."* **Romans 16:7 (NLT).**

♦ **Priscilla, the woman who instructed a man:** *"Now a certain Jew named Apollos, born at Alexandria, an eloquent man and mighty in the Scriptures, came to Ephesus. This man had been instructed in the way of the Lord; and being fervent in spirit, he spoke and taught accurately the things of the Lord, though he knew only the baptism of John. So, he began to speak boldly in the synagogue. <u>When Aquila and Priscilla heard him, they took him aside and explained to him the way of God more accurately."</u>* **Acts 18:24-26 (NKJV).**

Once again, we will place special emphasis on this last example due to two important aspects of it:

1. The order in which the names are mentioned in the Bible is relevant:

Because Priscilla's name is mentioned first in all the biblical references to this couple, some commentators have considered that her work in the Lord's work may have been much more outstanding than that of her husband.

As an example of this, we have the times that Paul and Silas were mentioned, since Paul was always named before his companion due to the notoriety of the former in relation to the latter.

2. Priscilla took part in the instruction:

The Bible clearly states that Priscilla, in the company of her husband, instructed the evangelist Apollos so that he could expound God's message more excellently. In other words, although she was a woman, she taught an eloquent male preacher like Apollos, which is further evidence that what is said in 1 Timothy 2:12 does not refer to the ministerial action of women but the divine order established by the Lord for husbands in their homes.

But our exposition on this subject would not be complete if we do not also highlight the fact that certainly in ancient times, there was a high level of oppression and prejudice against women to occupy a very inferior stratum to men in the ancient world.

To such an extent, that the Greek poet Sophocles came to say:

"Silence confers grace on women." While the Jews had an even lower idea of them, to such an extent that many sayings minimize their place in society in the Jewish Talmud. Let us see an example:

"As for teaching a woman the law, it is the same as teaching her impiety." "The same as casting pearls before swine, it is the same as teaching a woman the law." In addition to this, according to this same law, it was forbidden for a man to speak to a woman in the street or to ask her for any favor, even if it was his wife or his own daughter.

However, none of the above is above what the word of the Lord establishes, saying:

"There is no longer Jew or Gentile, slave or free, male and female. For you are all one in Christ Jesus." **Galatians 3:28 (NLT).**

However, if anyone dares to say that this passage only applies to salvation, then we would be saying that the blood of Christ could restore all things to their original state, except the woman, who, although certainly still under an order of subjection. But, as 1 Timothy 2:12 says, that subjection (as we have already seen) refers to the house affairs, not to those of the church. Therefore, the same must be applied according to the design traced on the part of God.

Although she was a woman, she taught an eloquent male preacher like Apollos.

Finally, let us consider the following: if God disapproves of the ministry of women...

How is it that women have been, and continue to be used to bring so many souls to the feet of Christ for so many years?

How can they be used to plant and develop churches the way they do?

How is it that millions are renewed through the message from their mouths, the captives are set free, and the weak in the faith are strengthened?

If it is not God, then who uses them, if the Bible clearly states that no kingdom divided against itself can stand (See Luke 11:17) and that unless the Lord builds the house, those who build it labor in vain. (See Psalms 127:1).

As far as we are concerned, we understand that God wastes nothing, so He would never have given the woman gifts, talents, and abilities that He was not willing to use because...

"Every good gift and every perfect gift are from above, and comes down from the Father of lights, with whom there is no variation or shadow of turning." **James 1:17 (NKJV).**

Chapter Principles

1. The creation of man, in the beginning, refers to the whole human race, although by then, it was contained within a single body, which was that of Adam.

2. God did not qualify the woman as an inferior being to man in making her but positioned her as his companion and complement.

3. It is God's design that man should marry, for marriage was instituted by Himself.

4. When the apostle instructed the church about the gifts of the Spirit, he said that "all," both men and women, can prophesy so that "all" men and women can learn and be comforted.

5. Although the gifts are present in a church, there is a need for mature leadership among those who have attained real growth and understanding in the Word of God. Because to be well-grounded, it is fundamental to maintain a balance between the moving of the Spirit and the handling of the Word.

6. According to God's order for the home, the woman has no "head" of her own but must be

united to the man, who is her head. But this does not refer to the rule of a carnal head, but to the headship of a man who, in turn, is guided by Christ, whose head is God.

7. God has deposited the responsibility of leadership in the home on the male "husband," but he must first allow himself to be guided by the guidance of Christ to fulfill the function of head of his wife, as has been established by the Lord.

8. Couples grounded in Christian values should set aside their own carnal sovereignties and properly implement the order established by God for the home.

9. Women can minister the Word in the church, but according to the order established by God, married women should let themselves be guided by their husbands and learn from them in the home, as long as they are guided by the one who should be their head, which is Jesus Christ.

10. God wastes nothing, so He would never have given women gifts, talents, and abilities He was unwilling to use.

Closing Words

Finally, never forget that in any situation that occurs to you, you can only make one of two decisions:

Either you allow yourself to be crushed by it, or you use it as a driving force to take you to the destiny that God has indicated for you. Therefore, make a good decision!

Do not give any prejudice, pressure, crisis, or downfall the power to slow you down, stall you or harm you because you are not a victim but a survivor. You are a woman marked by God to impact the generation you belong to. Therefore, do not let anything steal your essence. Reveal your design and take your rightful place as an overcomer.

"For we are His workmanship, created in Christ Jesus for good works, which God prepared beforehand that we should walk in them." Ephesians 2:10 (NKJV).

Other books from the author

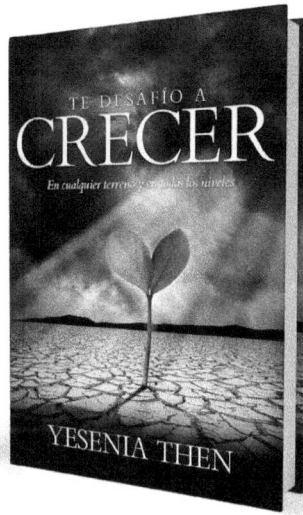

I Challenge You to Grow

More than a simple book, it is a tool of inspiration, direction, and empowerment that will make you not settle for less than what you were created to be. The challenge stands, dare to grow continuously above all your circumstances without being ruled by your difficulties.

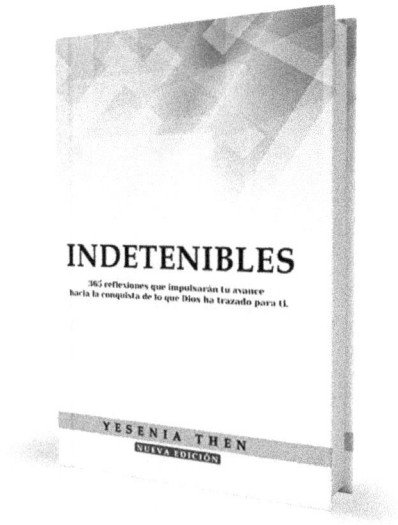

Unstoppable

365 messages, anecdotes, and illustrations that will propel you towards the conquest of what God has planned for you. With reading fragments loaded with impact, wisdom, and inspiration from God through its author, Yesenia Then. A book only recommended for those who do not accept any other design than the one God has already created for them and who, until they see that design fulfilled in their lives, have made the firm and obstinate decision to be UNSTOPPABLE.

Diamonds

It is an easy-to-read book that contains two hundred phrases of activation, inspiration, and instruction from God, which, if put into practice, will serve as a valuable tool to live more wisely, effectively, and productively the journey of life that lies before you.

www.ingramcontent.com/pod-product-compliance
Lightning Source LLC
Chambersburg PA
CBHW051423090426
42737CB00014B/2803

* 9 7 9 8 9 8 7 9 1 4 4 0 3 *